What Others Are Saying About This Book...

If there is *one* book to use as a guide to develop a successful business, this book is it. This is a truly special book that expresses basic truths about business and teaches how to easily and successfully implement those truths.

> *A. Thomas Connick, Esquire*
> *Private Attorney and Civic Activist*
> *1999 Recipient of The Florida Bar's*
> *President's Pro Bono Service Award*

Entrepreneurs require more than great business cards and a sound business plan. Emotional intelligence is the most vital asset in achieving success. For those who desire to reach higher ground through simple confidence building steps – *this* is a must-read book!

> *Gina Chiarenza, President*
> *APS ATM Processing Services, Inc.*

Having worked with Suzanne, I can say with confidence that her strategies for growing a successful business work. After implementing Suzanne's ideas and suggestions, I generated more revenue in three months than I did in the prior year. This book is filled with many of the strategies that helped me become successful.

> *Madeline Andrews*
> *President and CEO*
> *Model Millennium, Inc.*

D1695718

Suzanne has worked with many of our members as they transitioned from working for others to working for themselves. This book provides a quick look at many of the hurdles to be cleared as you become a true entrepreneur.

Dennis Grady
President
Chamber of Commerce
of the Palm Beaches

Suzanne is an advocate for entrepreneurs. She knows how to diminish the fears about growing a business by guiding the client's efforts with her vivacious encouragement and nonstop energy. For me, she is a combination of angel and cheerleader.

Rose Lee Archer
Producer and Host
Rose Lee Archer Show
Winner of the 2002 Women in Business
Advocate of the Year Award by the U.S.
Small Business Administration

No matter how successful you were in corporate America, you know nothing about becoming an entrepreneur. I know because I was the president/CEO of four companies before I became an entrepreneur. I could have used this book.

Sigmund Goodwin
Vice-President
The Radcliff Company

Employee to Entrepreneur

The Employee's Guide to Entrepreneurial Success

Suzanne Mulvehill, MBA

First Edition

Business Publications, Inc.
Delray Beach, Florida

Employee to Entrepreneur

Suzanne Mulvehill, MBA

Published by:
Business Publications, Inc.
Post Office Box 7154
Delray Beach, FL 33482
info@profit-strategies.com
www.profit-strategies.com
A division of Profit Strategies, Inc.

Editor: Lucy Chabot Reed
Proofreader: Patricia Patterson
Cover Design: Serena Hoermann, www.twofins.com
About the Cover: Photo courtesy of John Waibel, owner of Spirit of the West Adventures, www.kayak-adventures.com. It was during a 9-day kayak trip with John's company in British Columbia, Canada, that it became clear to me that I would be writing this book. This photo, which was from his brochure, was so memorable to me that a year later I contacted John to ask if I could use this photo for the cover of my book. When John realized that the photo was of him, he said, "How appropriate because I am an entrepreneur, too."

Printed in the United States of America

Library of Congress Control Number 2003090203

Mulvehill, Suzanne M.
    Employee to Entrepreneur: The Employee's Guide to Entrepreneurial Success / Suzanne M. Mulvehill. – 1st ed.

ISBN 0-9727565-0-7

1. Small Business   2. Entrepreneurship   3. New Business Enterprises

Bulk quantities of this book are available to corporations, universities, professional associations and other organizations. Please contact (561) 272-8004, FAX: (561) 272-1504 or (e-mail) info@profit-strategies.com

Dedication

For my parents, Joe and Hilda, who laid the foundation for my
life as an entrepreneur. I learned great things – and
continue to learn life lessons – from these two special people.

Table of Contents

Acknowledgements

I am grateful to all my clients who taught me so much about the process of entrepreneurship. I'd also like to acknowledge my friends, colleagues and business coaches who supported me along the way. Thank you my dear children, Chris and Melissa, for your patience and loving support while I worked on this book.

About this Book

Having worked with hundreds of entrepreneurs in all stages of personal and business development, I am convinced that people go through a transformation as they transition from being an employee to becoming an entrepreneur.

I was working as a business counselor for a Small Business Development Center when I realized that the majority of time I spent with each client was not counseling them on what I was contracted to do, helping them develop marketing strategies. The majority of time was spent helping them develop emotional stamina – learning how to be courageous, dealing with the discomfort of the transition, making necessary changes and overcoming the obstacles that were holding them back.

Behind closed doors each client revealed themselves – their vulnerability and fears. I connected to each and every client because I too had made the transition from employee to entrepreneur and had understood and overcome many of the challenges they were now dealing with.

Oddly enough, personal growth, while secondary to their purpose for seeing me, became their primary accomplishment. They grew for the sake of their business, in spite of their business and for their business. I nurtured and guided them while they felt joy, sorrow, fear, frustration, anger, exhaustion and just about every emotion in between. And as they worked through those emotions, their businesses grew.

My clients were becoming their true selves through this process. They were changing, both personally and professionally, from the inside out. Through this transforming experience, they realized that anything was possible with determination and belief.

I became aware that my clients' businesses grew in proportion to their personal growth. Those who focused on business growth without addressing personal growth stayed stuck where they were. Once they recognized that the key to their success was inside them, they became willing to grow personally to experience professional success.

I also recognized that anyone could decide to be an entrepreneur, as long as they had yearning and passion. For many, however, it is not so much a decision but a becoming. As one reaches a level of personal wholeness and growth, this yearning for an expression of oneself comes forth. If the yearning is denied, personal growth is denied. And so the struggle begins to allow this expression to be acknowledged and nurtured.

This transition to entrepreneurship existed whether one was in the idea phase, still had a job while starting a business or was running a business full-time. Some were challenged with dealing with the time before the money flows and remaining positive. Others were challenged with feeling they had to set up their company perfectly. Regardless of what challenge they were overcoming, all were learning how to live in the unknown, to be vulnerable and exposed, and at the same time willing to do whatever it took to become an entrepreneur and experience their lives in a new way.

Employee to Entrepreneur helps you deal with the emotions, fears and uncertainties of starting and running a business. It is designed to prepare you for a journey into the unknown, providing you with tools to transition from being an employee to becoming an entrepreneur. It is my belief that the lack of tools to deal with the emotional challenges of entrepreneurship is the primary reason that 50 percent of new businesses fail in the United States. Don't let yours be one of them.

How to Use this Book

This book is designed as a workbook with space for you to record your responses, commitments, affirmations and experiences. My personal journal entries are sited as an introduction to each exercise in the book to help you see the experience I went through and how my journey unfolded. Many of my clients' experiences are revealed in the exercises to help you see how they dealt with and overcame their challenges. Each exercise ends with an affirmation that supports you in your journey.

The challenges described require action – be it mental, emotional, physical or spiritual. You will be encouraged to expand yourself and practice self-discipline. If you want to get a lot out of the experience and be transformed, put a lot of you and your time into it.

Since each of you is at a different stage of your entrepreneurial journey, I suggest you start this book at whatever challenge you are experiencing. If you want to start a business but don't know where to begin, start at Challenge One. If you are in business and having trouble dealing with the time before the money flows, start with Challenge Seven. Once you complete the challenge that is most difficult for you, then go back and start the book from the beginning.

You can go at your own pace or work the challenges with a partner or support person. Expect to feel your feelings, all of them. They are a vital part of this journey, even the uncomfortable ones.

Be free to live and be the greatest expression of who you are.

INTRODUCTION

My Story

As far back as I can remember I worked in jobs where I had a job description and followed rules and instructions. I made a living and had a nice life. What else could I want?

In 1995, I began yearning to be my own boss. I didn't understand it and I didn't know what kind of business I wanted to start. This was a new feeling for me. I had just completed three years of school and earned my master's in business administration degree. I had accepted an executive-level position and made a nice salary.

On some level, I knew that connecting with my higher self through entrepreneurship was the next step, though I talked myself out of making this transition for several years. I wasn't clear about what I wanted to do so I told myself that I'd wait until my kids were grown, until I had more money, got a new car or a new house.

This desire to be my own boss wouldn't leave me and as scary as it was, I acknowledged my desire, and became willing to move through the experience. I realized that for me, the process of letting go of my job and stepping into new territory was more difficult than any change I had experienced in my life.

I started a journal, writing down ideas for businesses and just fantasizing about what it would be like to be my own boss. I read *Entrepreneur Magazine* and attended business seminars. I continued working and making more money. I was comfortable, so why wouldn't this yearning leave me?

I stayed in this emotional state for two years, accepting a position for another company and advancing three times over the next year and a half. My journal began to reveal new ideas such as launching a magazine, writing a book, and being a consultant. I realized that my inner voice was farther ahead of my emotional self.

When I was promoted the third time, I had to take a test to prove my worth. Although my boss and I both knew that the test did not accurately measure my skill level, he decided to believe the results of the test. The promotion was taken away as fast as I got it.

I was told that the company was willing to train me and in the mean time I would be given a salary increase and a different title for the job I was already doing. I felt slighted and turned it down. No amount of money, no job title or promotion was worth losing my value as a person. The next day I gave my notice. I realized that I stood up for myself in a way I never had before. I felt a new sense of bravery.

A few days later, I surprised myself by accepting a job in a different division – not because I wanted the job but because I was afraid. My belief that I needed a paycheck to live was so strong that it took precedence over all else. I realized that working for someone was the only style of work I had ever known. I began to wonder if I could really change.

This whole process of trying to leave my job was emotionally draining – I constantly questioned myself and knew that I was buying time until I could find the courage to leave for good. I wasn't even going to look for another job. I had allowed my jobs to take away my uniqueness, my individuality and my self-esteem. These feelings pushed me into my entrepreneurial desires. That scared me, too. What I really wanted to do I didn't know, but I knew that I needed to do something, to just start somewhere.

After several years of having ideas of what I wanted to do as an entrepreneur, I made a decision that I felt was the best I could make at that time. I decided to publish a magazine. I had been in the publishing industry for a few years and liked it. I understood the industry, had numerous contacts within it and had identified a niche market for my magazine.

I read some business books, investigated local business development programs and went to S.C.O.R.E., Service Corps of Retired Executives, a division of the U.S. Small Business

Administration to get guidance on becoming a small business owner. All the books I read, people I met and seminars I attended summarized how to get started as a small business owner quite simply – write a business plan, work in an area familiar to you, and have at least six months of savings before leaving your job. "I can do that," I thought. I established a budget, began researching the market and putting my plan together.

Five months after my first failed attempt to leave my job, I was ready once again. Only this time I had a business plan and savings. I gave my notice and fear set in again. I didn't understand it – I had a plan, I saved money, I followed the guidelines of starting a business – but I felt the same fears I had when I gave in and accepted my job back the first time.

Over the next few days I still planned to leave my job, but fear was overwhelming me. I felt sick to my stomach, dizzy a lot of the time and somewhat disoriented. It was as if this change – which I wanted to make – was a shock to my body. I even had dreams about being out of control.

I was again offered some variations in my job and I accepted. I was happy to be relieved of these uncomfortable feelings. Having attempted to leave my job twice now in six months, I felt trapped. I was tortured by my thoughts: What was it going to take? Was I ever going to leave this job? How come I couldn't leave? What was wrong with me? Why do I have to leave? Why can't I stay at this job since I'm doing so well at it?

I reflected on the two times that I tried to leave my job and realized something important. I hadn't done anything to change me. All of my efforts in becoming an entrepreneur were outside of me – writing a business plan, saving money and focusing on gaining business knowledge. My thoughts and fears were still the same, my beliefs were the same and my insecurities were the same. So I asked to myself, "What do I need to do now?" The answer, of course, was "change and grow."

I realized that the preparation I needed to make before I could resign the next time was inside me. I came to understand that a business plan or savings were not the key to becoming an entrepreneur. The key was that I needed to be willing to take on my fears and change my way of thinking about my future. I needed to come face-to-face with my fears, insecurities, likes and dislikes. I needed to get to know me. Yes, a business plan and savings were important to me but more important was that I could learn how to accept change in my life. I needed to prepare emotionally, mentally and spiritually for this transition.

I became aware of my patterns and behaviors and began to understand why I was unable to leave my job. I didn't know how to be OK with uncertainty. My self-confidence and self-esteem, which I thought were within me, were actually "on loan" to me from my employer. I had come to rely on my employer to provide my sense of security.

I wanted so badly to change that I began working as diligently on myself as I had on my business plan. I accepted that I was afraid. I searched out mental blocks within myself and wrote them down. I admitted my fear of success, fear of failure and began talking to friends. I was getting to the root of my discomfort – dealing and living with the unknown. I slowly opened my mind to accept my fear of the unknown. The personal growth I was working toward helped me shift my thinking and I began to become comfortable with uncertainty – as uncomfortable as it was.

I realized that moving out of my comfort zone was a process and that I could expand myself by doing things I had never done. I didn't have to wait until I left my job. I expanded my mind by allowing the unknown to become my friend rather than my enemy. Here, the unknown was available to me every day and I didn't even know it until I looked for it. I took every opportunity I could imagine to do things differently. I realized that I had never valet parked, so I tried it. I always walked my dog one way around the block, so I walked her the other way. I got up earlier than I was used to. I ordered food that I never ordered before. I began to change my patterns and feel the discomfort of change in everyday activities. I became aware of my habits and how engrained they were in me. And I consciously began to make changes.

Over the next four months, I wrote affirmations on index cards and I read books about inner strength. I strengthened my relationship with myself and with God. I humbled myself, realizing that I needed spiritual guidance to make the break from this job. I went through so many emotions during this time. It was grueling. I struggled with thoughts that I might go crazy or be crazy if I really did leave this job. I wondered if there was something wrong with me for feeling I needed to leave.

I again needed to decide what I would do as an entrepreneur. This time I didn't put together a business plan. I just made some strategic decisions about what I wanted to do. I gave up on the idea of publishing a magazine. I didn't have the capital and didn't want to spend the energy to get it. I evaluated my skills and realized that I really enjoyed helping companies succeed – that was what I did best. I also knew that I wanted to start a business without a lot of startup capital and that I wanted to promote my skills to my existing customer base. So I decided to keep this process simple and start out by positioning myself as a consultant.

I planned for about two months the date that I would give my notice and prepared myself for this day. I began to create the plan and the vision – I would leave my job in mid-November, take the month of December off and start a consulting project in January.

When mid-November came, I again gave notice. It was four months after my last attempt to leave my job. I was scared that I would fall back into my familiar pattern. But this time, I felt different. I didn't have all of those scary and uncomfortable feelings. I became used to change – it wasn't a shock to my body anymore and I felt remarkably calm and serene.

I made it to "the other side" and began entering new territory, full of uncertainty. I felt so relieved about having done what I couldn't do twice before. I began to feel a new sense of freedom. I felt deep feelings of fulfillment in my life and recognized how much I had grown. I felt secure within myself and was awestruck as to how all the work I did on myself culminated into feelings of self-assuredness, the ability to let go of what was familiar, and the ability to feel OK with uncertainty. While I was still afraid, my fears were not crippling me anymore.

I prayed a lot during this time. I found it helpful to surround myself with people who were doing what I wanted to do and talked to a lot of supportive friends to help me feel confident that I wouldn't go back. I was learning how to simply "be." I was OK.

New, uncomfortable feelings surfaced after this initial "honeymoon" phase of feeling the relief from leaving my job. The first time I felt these new uncomfortable feelings was at a holiday party. I found that I didn't have my job to talk about anymore and didn't know what to talk about. I felt kind of weird in this "in between" space of not knowing where I was going on this entrepreneurial journey. I came to realize that these uncomfortable feelings were just additional opportunities for me to grow and I accepted them as such. Fear was not the prevailing emotion any longer – willingness was. I was willing to grow through these changes as they came up and learned that I had many options. I could learn new skills; ask for help and request spiritual guidance.

My friend Gina, who had started a business that same year, had her business inside a business incubator. She was her own boss and I admired her for living the life I desired. I went to visit her at the business incubator in January. She told me that the coordinator of the incubator program had just left and the incubator needed a re-vamping. Gina said, "Suzanne, this would be a great consulting project for you." From that moment on, things happened very quickly. The director of the program invited me into his office to discuss the possibility of me contracting to help the incubator. I negotiated a rate, established the number of hours I would work and determined the time span for the project.

I started this consulting project before I even had business cards. I went to the library to see about setting up a contract, wrote one up and I started working the following Monday. I began to trust this uncertainty thing. It was working. I didn't understand it, but that didn't matter. I was moving in the direction I wanted to move in. I continued to expand my everyday life by trying new things and expanding my world of uncertainty.

I discovered that getting and doing business was somehow different now that I was on my own. I didn't have to meet hundreds of people to get clients. In my prior job, I would make 250 sales calls a week and book 15-20 appointments to build my sales. I worked myself to the bone to get business. Somehow, working on my own was different. New opportunities presented themselves in strange, coincidental ways.

Through the financial highs and lows of the first two years, I was tormented by fear of success, of failure and of not making enough money. I told myself I could always go back and get another job. From time to time, my old boss called to see if I wanted my job back. His calls actually gave me confidence. I realized that I wasn't stuck, that I was choosing my entrepreneurial lifestyle – the good times and the bad – and that I was making it, even if I was challenged financially. His calls also helped me realize that I was still employable and could always go back and get a paycheck if I really needed one.

I continued to get new projects. Some I turned down and some I accepted. I learned to trust the process of entrepreneurship. In my third year, a colleague asked if I'd be interested in a marketing director's position for an international company. The pay was about three times what I was earning as an entrepreneur but I didn't have to think twice. I said, "Thank you for the offer but no." I realized that money didn't come first. It never really did, but now I was certain that my needs came before any financial prospects. I wasn't going to sacrifice myself for money anymore, even if that meant eating macaroni and cheese for dinner instead of steak.

I finally realized that going back to being an employee was a choice, not a necessity, and the success I was seeking was inside me all along.

**Go confidently in the direction of your dreams!
Live the life you have imagined.**

Henry David Thoreau

CHALLENGE I
GETTING THE GUTS

I sure think a lot about starting a business. I wonder if this is something I'd really like to do. I think I would – but would I? Could I? There's something in me that craves more than a job.

How do you get the guts to go off on your own and leave what you know – be it the security of a job, a career or a paycheck? Most people get the guts when they become brave and courageous and are willing to step out in the unknown.

Bravery and courage are learned behaviors. We learn how to become brave by taking action. It is in becoming brave in small ways that we become brave in big ways.

Brave and courageous acts are available to us every moment. We need to look for ways to be brave. We must be committed to getting the guts – to becoming brave and courageous. This challenge focuses on choosing to be brave consciously – choosing to do things differently and experience our lives in new ways.

Welcome bravery and courage into your life, into your being. Take action and get the guts to become the entrepreneur you want to be. Be brave – you are experiencing the transition of a lifetime!

**Courageous risks are life giving,
they help you grow, make you brave and better
than you think you are.**

Joan L. Curio

Make a Conscious Choice

I am ready to make some changes – to experience some change in my personal and professional life.

Make a conscious choice to start this journey. Simply begin exactly where you are. It is like going to college in the sense that you may not know exactly what you want to do when you finish, but you know that you will find out along the way. Entrepreneurship is similar; you learn as you go. You don't need to have all the answers now, today or tomorrow. They will come to you as you need them. Make a conscious choice simply to begin. This is the first step to becoming brave and getting the guts to achieve what you desire. It lets you and your energy know that you are making a commitment to be brave and courageous, even if you don't know what it is that you want to do yet.

This does not mean you need to quit your job or change anything at the moment. All it means is that you are making a commitment to be brave and courageous as you begin your entrepreneurial journey.

Write your commitment to be brave and courageous:

_____

_____

_____

_____

Today, I am making a conscious choice to be brave.

Let The Journey Begin!

God willing, I am going to start a business.

If you want to start a business – start it. If you want to expand your business, expand it. Start in some small way doing what you want to be doing. Begin allowing that part of you – that part that wants to experience life in the way you desire – to express itself. Too often, we think we need to wait for exactly the right time to start, launch or even begin exploring what it is we want to do, while in reality there really is no such thing as the "exact right time."

One day I wondered what I would do if I won the lottery. I wrote it all down: I would buy a Ford Explorer, I would start my own business and I would spend more time with my children. What I learned was that I didn't have to wait until I won the lottery. I began to do the things on my lottery list without winning. Waiting for the lottery was not the answer. Being courageous to live the life I desired was.

What would you be doing if you won the lottery, if money were not a concern?

_____

_____

_____

_____

_____

_____

In what ways will you begin now? Will you attend the seminar you've been wanting to attend? Make a decision about something? Start a business plan? Meet with a business counselor? List ways you can begin taking action right now.

_____

_____

_____

_____

| *I am beginning now – right where I am.* |

Rekindle Your Entrepreneurial Spirit

*Somebody asked me again today if I am a teacher and I said no.
I wonder why people ask me that.*

We were created as entrepreneurs to use our talents and share them with the world. Somehow we knew this as children: baking and selling cookies, setting up lemonade stands. Many of us simply forgot along the way.

Looking back over my life, I had more entrepreneurial spirit from the ages of five to ten than I did for the next twenty years. When did the entrepreneurial spirit leave the girl who collected, painted and sold seashells from the Jersey shore? The entrepreneurial spirit left me when I traded it for the security of a job. It wasn't until I decided to become an entrepreneur that I realized that I lacked creativity and needed to rekindle my entrepreneurial spirit.

Describe how you were entrepreneurial growing up. What did you do to express your creativity, your entrepreneurial spirit? Did you invent something? Play games with rules that you made up? Draw? Paint? Sell your hand-painted works of art?

_____

_____

_____

_____

_____

Now, look back over what you wrote and see if anything that you did as a child is what you want to be doing as an entrepreneur. What we are looking for is an underlying theme. One of my passions as a young child was to teach imaginary children the subject of math. A small section of the basement of my home was set up as my classroom. The only reality in this classroom was a chalkboard, chalk, eraser and a few chairs.

I spent hours there teaching. I can still recall the enjoyment I felt doing it. I loved it. How does this relate to my entrepreneurial spirit as an adult? The more I allowed my entrepreneurial spirit to come forth as an adult, the more I recognized my desire to give seminars and to teach. Eventually, seminars and training became a core component of my business.

What did you love to do as a child that you would like to be doing now?

_____

_____

_____

Another way to rekindle to your entrepreneurial spirit is through moments when you knew something just felt right. These moments can be subtle but at the same time, you knew they were telling you something. When I was in the third year of my MBA program, I walked to the podium to give a presentation and had the feeling I would do this a lot in the future. I didn't think that was possible at the time because I felt so uncomfortable giving presentations. Now, years later, I realize that feeling was valid. I give presentations and workshops on a consistent basis and am a member of the National Speakers Association.

Describe moments from your past when you got that feeling that something was right for you, even if you did not understand it.

_____

_____

_____

Does any of what you described above play a role in what you are looking to do as an entrepreneur? If so, describe below. I recall several people in my life who asked me if I was a teacher. I told them "no" because my thought of a teacher was a person who teaches school. I had not yet realized that there are many kinds of teachers, and that I was one of them.

_____

_____

_____

I nurture my entrepreneurial spirit.

Get to Know What is Going on "Inside" You – Start Journaling

My journal – how it calls me – or I call for it. For me, journaling is just as important as eating or sleeping. It's a necessity in my life – a way to move through – to process – to move beyond the ordinary.

Begin journaling. No judgment – just journaling. No excuses now. I've heard them all, including, "I was forced to write as a child and now I don't like writing." It takes courage to get to know ourselves so we can experience our lives in a new way.

Buy yourself a notebook or something you would enjoy writing in. You might like writing on notebook paper or you may prefer a colorful journal. Whatever it is, just make sure it has plenty of blank pages. Some say it is best to journal when you wake up. I prefer journaling at night. Try both and see what works best for you. I suggest you write in your journal at least five days a week.

Take time each day to jot down your feelings, your accomplishments, your challenges, what you enjoyed and how you participated in life. Your journaling does not have to relate specifically to your business or your ideas but rather your feelings and experiences in everyday life. The point is to write honestly and get to know yourself. Write your goals and dreams. Write about yourself; get to know yourself on a deeper level than ever before. Your relationship with your self is the most important relationship you have on this journey.

Why is journaling so important? Because we develop courage and confidence as we get to know ourselves and grow personally and professionally. When we journal, we can see and feel and experience our progress.

Journaling is a key to my progress.

15

Welcome Your Ideas

Idea: create seminars/workshops called "Taking the Leap" – emotional, mental and spiritual preparation for leaving the security of a job and venturing into the world of entrepreneurship. (This idea came three years before the thought of writing a book on this subject.)

Whenever a client comes to me with an idea, it is theirs, unique to them. Ideas are seedlings to your heart – to your dream. They lead you to where you want to go, especially if you do not know what you want to do.

It takes courage to let your ideas come forth and begin acting on them. I worked with a physician who wanted to leave his practice and open a retail store. Even though he loved his idea of opening a retail store, he struggled with being brave and taking action on implementing his idea. He had not yet developed the courage to do what he wanted to do instead of what society said he "should" do. I shared with him that entrepreneurship is for the brave. Unfortunately, he stopped coming to business counseling and I never heard from him again.

Write down some of your ideas to start or enhance your business.

1. _____

2. _____

3. _____

4. _____

5. _____

6. _____

7. _____

8. _____

9. _____

10. _____

Look back over the ideas you've written down. Write down next to each idea how long you've had it.

The goal of this exercise is to courageously express different ideas. The business you may pursue may be an extension of one of the ideas you've listed. I discovered that many of the ideas I wrote down over the years led me to my business. It was a process of trial and error – letting some ideas go and deciding to pursue others. I saw certain themes in the ideas I expressed that, looking back, were indicators as to what I truly wanted to do.

Elaborate on your ideas in your journal. Simply write down what idea you have and whatever else comes to you at that moment. You can expand on any idea you like, research the market, explore competition, etc. What we are looking for here is where your creativity leads you. The goal is not to act on any particular idea at this time but to simply be aware of what ideas you have and get them flowing. Your creative side will love this exercise because as it gets acknowledged and is respected by you, it will reveal more clarity and direction to you.

Be brave! Write down your creative ideas, regardless of what they are.

I value all of my ideas.

Build Courage

I am scared to death but excited as hell. I am quitting my job today.

Eleanor Roosevelt once said, "You must do the thing that you think you cannot do." It takes courage to do something we think we cannot do, to make a change we are unsure of, to start an entrepreneurial journey. It takes courage to do things differently. Courage is the ability to feel afraid and do what needs to be done anyway.

Courage is important in our personal and professional lives. When we work at building and developing courage, it protects us and strengthens our self-image and self-esteem. Courage gives us a "Wow, I can do that" feeling. Recently, I completed a full-day planning session with a client. I was scared, excited and nervous, but I did it and I got to benefit from not only enjoying the experience but also from feeling courageous – doing something that scared me. Building courage is done in small steps with circumstances that present themselves to us or that we choose to be in.

Courage requires action. What is courageous for one person may be easy for another. We can build and strengthen our ability to be courageous each time we do something that we didn't want to do, we thought we couldn't do or were afraid to do. Courage is the reward for doing something that we thought was impossible.

Act as if….

Acting as if means to act as if you have courage even if you do not. Acting as if is a valuable technique for building courage, particularly for practicing new responses to old and familiar circumstances. Nina worked on developing courage by acting as if she was courageous. She was intelligent, recently completed a master's in business administration degree and started her own business selling promotional products. She learned everything she needed to start the business, but that didn't help her develop courage. She shared that she felt inexperienced and awkward in her new role as an entrepreneur. She was brave enough to ask, "How do I get the courage to go out on a cold call and meet potential clients?" I told her about the "act as if" concept – to simply act as if she felt courageous. In essence, it is like tricking your mind into believing that you feel courageous so you can take the action you need or desire to take. This exercise helped Nina make cold calls and sell her products.

Describe situations that scare you or that you do not want to do but know that you must. You will know that they are situations you need to address because you may be putting them off or feel scared whenever you think of them. These are the situations this exercise calls for, situations that can be used to build courage. For example, is there someone you need to confront about an issue that is bothering you? Have you wanted to incorporate your business but haven't? Describe a situation below.

Situation 1:

_____

_____

_____

Describe how you can "act as if" you are courageous:

_____

_____

_____

Situation 2:

_____

_____

_____

Describe how you can "act as if" you are courageous:

_____

_____

_____

Situation 3:

_____

_____

_____

Describe how you can "act as if" you are courageous:

_____

_____

_____

Now comes the action part. "Act as if" you are courageous and take action on each situation you described above. Know that it might feel awkward. That is OK. Remember, to build courage we need to take action. Once you completed the "act as if" action for each situation, describe below how you felt taking action and being courageous.

_____

_____

_____

Read your response above each time you need to remember the results from acting courageous. I find this exercise very helpful. Sometimes when I need courage to speak to a large group of people and feel like I need courage, I read what I wrote the last time I gave a talk to a large group and felt courageous. Courage builds courage! It works – every time.

The reason this building courage exercise is so important is because if we have not worked on building courage into our lives, we may not have the stamina to withstand our entrepreneurial journey and will turn back. That is what happened to me. I returned to my job two times after giving notice because I had not worked at building courage into my life. I didn't realize how important courage was until I didn't have the courage to leave my job. It wasn't until I practiced building courage that I was able to leave my job for good.

I am courageous.

Develop Confidence

I've spent the past seven years improving my professional skills and I feel confident in what I do.

Confidence is a positive feeling in ourselves and is an integral part of starting and operating a business. The challenge with confidence is two-fold: virtually everything we do as a new business owner requires confidence and we need to have confidence even though we do not have accomplishments yet as an entrepreneur. Therefore, developing confidence, rather than just relying on the confidence we have, is essential to becoming an entrepreneur.

Confidence can no longer come from a paycheck, a title, an office, a boss or anything outside of ourselves. Confidence is developed within ourselves over time. Often, as a new business owner, we may look for financial rewards to help us develop confidence. Usually, if that is all we rely on, our business will not survive. As we develop confidence in ourselves, we will naturally develop confidence in our business.

One way to develop confidence is to believe in ourselves – to simply make the decision to believe. Believing in ourselves is at the core of confidence. We recognize our strengths and weaknesses and acknowledge ourselves as human beings. We need to be patient and gentle with ourselves while we develop confidence.

We can develop our confidence by recognizing and acknowledging our feelings, being courageous and acting as if we feel confident. When we take action on an issue or situation that scares us, we benefit from being courageous by feeling confident. I saw many clients develop confidence in this way.

We need to look for opportunities to develop confidence. These opportunities include recognizing our accomplishments – small and large. We make a conscious effort to see our progress.

Since confidence is a feeling, we can create a confident feeling through a mind-altered state by changing our thinking. When we alter our thinking, we create mind-altered confidence. It may be temporary, but it can get us through challenging or difficult situations. I altered my thinking by reading affirmations or envisioning my future and truly believing that this mind-altered state was already happening. This mind-altered state is created similarly to how coaches rally their teams before a game.

You often hear players huddle and yell out phrases together – that builds their confidence and creates a mind-altered state.

Stress is a confidence stealer. Be careful to avoid stressful situations and watch that you do not create stressful situations. We can create stressful situations by being late, not taking time to prepare, not getting adequate rest or not eating properly.

Each exercise below will help you develop confidence.

Acknowledge your accomplishments

Feelings of confidence are created when we acknowledge our accomplishments. We can maintain feelings of confidence by recognizing and acknowledging our accomplishments on a regular basis.

What accomplishments are you proud of? We are not looking for earth-shattering things here. We are looking for the accomplishments that made you feel good about yourself. Write down the accomplishments that you feel good about.

1. _____

2. _____

3. _____

4. _____

5. _____

Now comes the tough part for many – accepting compliments from others. Accepting compliments is important to developing and maintaining feelings of confidence. When we accept a compliment we are acknowledging our effort, our confidence. So often we disregard our accomplishments by not accepting compliments from others. Have you ever had someone say to you, "Great job!" and you responded with, "Oh, it was nothing really?" Or did you respond in some way that negated the compliment? Practice accepting compliments. When you accept a compliment, you are accepting confidence. It is in accepting compliments that we build confidence. Accepting a compliment is taking it in – saying thank you and appreciating your efforts being recognized. Find your own words to accept the compliment. Write down the next five compliments you hear from others that you accepted.

1. _____

2. _____

3. _____

4. _____

5. _____

Creating a mind-altered state is another exercise that is useful for building confidence. Usually we can create a mind-altered state by writing down and then repeating a phrase or a series of phrases that make us feel good about ourselves. What statements can you repeat to yourself to help you feel confident and overshadow your feelings of intimidation? Let these thoughts run on as you write them below. Do not stop and read them until you are finished writing. Don't judge or think about what you are writing; just write what comes to you. For example, "I love to share my message with others by speaking and presenting. I am a great speaker. My speaker participants love what I share and often tell me so. I have a great message to share and am looking forward to sharing it."

_____

_____

_____

Go back up over what you wrote and repeat it to yourself – read it at least two times and then write how you feel below. This exercise will help you realize that you can create a mind-altered state when you need to and have confidence that it will work for you.

_____

_____

_____

_____

| *I have confidence in myself and in my abilities.* |

Start Doing What You Like

It's true. Each time I do something new or different – I feel more courageous. It's like putting another feather in my cap.

What would you like to do that you have thought about for a long time but haven't done? This may be something extravagant, or it could be small and seemingly insignificant. By doing something that you know you would like to do but haven't done or haven't done in a long time, you are choosing to be brave – choosing to try something new and different. Consciously choosing to do something that you want to do takes courage.

I love to scuba dive, yet for 17 years, I didn't dive. I stopped doing what I liked doing and thus missed opportunities to be courageous. I decided to take diving lessons again five years ago and it was scary to learn how to dive again. I found that I needed more courage than the first time I learned how to dive. But I kept diving. I started my business a year after I started diving again. It is no coincidence that by being courageous and doing what I wanted to do in one area of my life – even if it was scary – allowed me to build courage in doing what I wanted in another.

What do you like to do or want to do but are not doing? You do not have to come up with any excuses for yourself or your circumstance. This exercise is about finding opportunities to be brave. Write down and begin to do what you know you would like to do, or want to do, but are not.

1. _____

2. _____

3. _____

4. _____

5. _____

I am courageous when I try new things.

Stop Doing What You Don't Like

I hate preparing budgets and here I am still doing them. No one even knows that I don't like doing this job. It's time for me to speak up, be brave and stop doing what I don't like doing.

What do you continue to do that you don't like to do? Although this sounds like an easy question with an easy answer, it often is not. I continued to work in jobs that I did not like because it was easier than being courageous and making a change. I didn't know how to be brave. I did not know it was courageous to stop doing what I did not like or at least start by saying that I did not like it. While it was easier to just continue doing what I did not like to do, I missed out on opportunities to be brave and to know myself better. Just because I was successful in these jobs didn't mean I liked them.

In order to make the big change of transitioning into entrepreneurship, I needed to make small changes first. I needed to practice being brave. I stopped attending evening business meetings and working nights. I told my boss I didn't like preparing the budgets and eventually that job was delegated to someone else.

What are your opportunities to be brave – to stop doing what you do not want to be doing? If it is something that you cannot stop doing immediately, what do you know you do not like doing that you would be willing to stop?

1. _____

2. _____

3. _____

4. _____

What actions will you take to stop doing what you do not want to do or do not like to do?

_____

_____

I am committed to stop doing things I do not like to do.

Go Places You Haven't Gone Before

I got the guts to pack up the car, drive to North Carolina and go camping with my kids. I felt so courageous doing something I wanted to do that I never did before.

We can become so used to our routines that we miss out on opportunities to be courageous by exploring new places. When we go to new places, we build courage.

Another benefit of going to new places is that you can get fresh ideas and revitalize your energy. Step back from the business or business idea and experience a new place. It doesn't matter if it is 15 minutes away or a day away. Just begin to experience new places and new situations. I recently broke away from my bicycling routine and found beautiful park just minutes from my house.

Go somewhere you haven't gone before. Take a vacation to a new place. I have seen clients experience great insight through vacations to new places. One client created the tagline for her business while sitting in an airport waiting for a flight. Stepping outside or being outside of our everyday surroundings helps us experience newness. And when we experience newness, we experience courage.

Let yourself be courageous. Where have you always wanted to go but haven't taken the time to go? When will you go? This destination can be a bike route in your neighborhood, a kayak trip across the country or a trip to an art museum. New places can be found minutes from your house, a few hours away or a few days away. Where can you go to experience newness and courage?

1. _____

2. _____

3. _____

4. _____

5. _____

Go back over the above list and write down a date upon which you plan to explore each new place. If you don't know where you would like to go, listen to yourself, especially when you first wake up. That is when my inner voice is usually the loudest. And that is when new ideas are just lingering there. Listen to your inner voice for a few days and then return to this exercise.

When I experience newness, I experience courage.

Put Those Goals In Writing!

I put my goals in writing today. It felt good – it felt courageous.
Now, I'll start accomplishing them, one at a time.

So many times, I asked clients if they had goals and they responded, "Yes, I have goals but they are all in my head." That means that they never wrote them down. Their first assignment was to put those goals in writing.

Here are the benefits of putting your goals in writing. First, you have the benefit of making a commitment to yourself. When you make a commitment to yourself, you have the opportunity to work toward accomplishing a goal – which builds courage and confidence. Second, you can feel confident in knowing that you have a plan of action. You know what you want to accomplish and you have it in writing.

When we set goals as entrepreneurs, we need to consider both our personal and professional goals. By setting personal goals in addition to professional goals, the business grows in the direction you desire. For example, Paul's personal goal was to have a flexible schedule so he could pick his children up from school and take them to their activities. He created his professional goals around this personal goal.

Entrepreneurs are often concerned about the business taking on a life of its own and being a slave to it – working day and night. Yes, this can happen, but only if you let it and if goals and boundaries are not set up prior to reaching extremes. In the event that business reaches a point of unmanageability, take a "time out" and reprioritize your goals.

When we don't have goals or have them but they are not prioritized, we can lose our focus. This is why Madeline came to see me for business counseling. Madeline owned a modeling agency and needed help setting goals. Her homework after our first meeting was to list her goals. Just to list them. It didn't matter how many she had. If she had a goal, she wrote it down. Madeline and I went over each goal and made sure each was measurable, time sensitive and realistic.

Consider the following questions as you begin to set your goals:

1. Is the goal measurable? Can you measure the results of the goal? For example, initially, Madeline's goal was to get new customers. How many did she want? One, five, ten? Without a specific number the goal

was not clearly defined. She decided she wanted to get ten new customers.

2. <u>Is the goal time sensitive?</u> Over what time frame will the goal be accomplished? In the example above, Madeline's goal was to generate ten new customers. She decided she could generate ten new customers in three months.

3. <u>Is the goal realistic?</u> Do you feel confident about your ability to achieve this goal? In the example with Madeline's goal of generating ten new customers in three months, she felt that goal was realistic. If your goal isn't realistic, refocus on questions 1 and 2.

List your goals:

1. _____

2. _____

3. _____

4. _____

5. _____

6. _____

7. _____

8. _____

9. _____

10. _____

Now that you have listed the goals you want to accomplish, prioritize them. What needs to happen first, second, third? Is there a sequence to what you are working to accomplish? Do this exercise with a friend or colleague. Ask for their input as you formulate the order of your goals.

Rewrite the previous list in a sequential order. For example, Madeline realized that her first goal was to get new customers – so she prioritized her list to make sure that all of the goals that related to getting new customers were before any other goals.

1. _____

2. _____

3. _____

4. _____

5. _____

6. _____

7. _____

8. _____

9. _____

10. _____

Many times I have worked with people who stop the goal-setting process once they've set their goals. I ask them, "How are you going to accomplish this goal? What steps need to take place to actually accomplish this goal?" Once you set a goal, the steps need to be defined as to how the goal will be accomplished.

Think about setting a goal to make $100,000 next year. OK, you've set a goal. But setting this goal is not enough to make it a reality. You need to define what needs to take place to reach this goal.

Let's go back to Madeline. Now that Madeline set the goal of generating ten new customers within three months, what steps does she need to set to reach this goal? What marketing efforts would she use? What sales techniques would she use? What did she need to do to generate ten new customers? For Madeline, the Web site was an important resource, so one of the steps to achieve this goal was to keep her Web site up to date with photos of new models. Another step was to send photos of new models to potential clients on a bi-weekly basis. A sample of her goal and the steps she set to accomplish this goal is below:

Goal 1: Get at least ten new customers over the next three months.

1. *Update the Web site bi-weekly with photos of new models.*

2. *Send announcements of new models to potential clients and current clients on a bi-weekly basis.*

3. *Create a direct mail piece within the next two weeks and send to at least 250 photographers.*

4. *Create an order tracking worksheet and a sales sheet to track calls and customer relations.*

For each of the goals listed in the previous exercise, describe the steps you need to take to accomplish each goal. The steps, just like the goals, need to be time sensitive, measurable and realistic.

Goal: _____

1. _____

2. _____

3. _____

4. _____

Goal: _____

1. _____

2. _____

3. _____

4. _____

Goal: _____

1. _____

2. _____

3. _____

4. _____

Goal: _____

1. _____

2. _____

3. _____

4. _____

Goal: _____

1. _____

2. _____

3. _____

4. _____

A year after setting, prioritizing and working toward her goals, Madeline's business generated more revenue in one quarter than it had the entire previous year. Goal setting works.

I build confidence and courage when I set and achieve goals.

Don't Give Up!

This is hard. Sometimes I feel like giving up, but then I think to myself, "What am I going to do go, back and do what I always did?" When I realize that I don't want to go backward, I push forward.

If you can imagine and feel it, you can work toward achieving it. Each step we take in working toward what we want builds courage. Don't give up. I counseled a man who would not give up. He created a product that could save lives. For years he refined his product while he worked small jobs. He cut out newspaper articles of people who died who would have lived had they used his product. He was financially poor and didn't have strong business skills but that didn't stop him. He kept pushing on and courageously taking one step forward at a time. The one time he did get a contract to install his product, he got injured and lacked financial resources to fulfill his contractual obligations.

Again, he didn't give up. He recognized that he needed to improve his business skills so he came in for business counseling. He and I worked on preparing a letter to several companies that might consider reviewing his product. The review and approval from one of these companies would be another step in helping him get his product to market.

A few months later, we met again. While many companies rejected his idea, one agreed to review it. This was a huge accomplishment and another step in the right direction. The approval from this company would mean an opportunity to sell his idea to a manufacturer or perhaps locate an investor. This letter let him know that he was moving closer to saving lives with his product.

Write your commitment to work toward your goals and not give up. Refer to this commitment whenever you need courage or confidence in your entrepreneurial journey.

_____

_____

_____

I am committed to get the guts.

GETTING THE GUTS
CHALLENGE REVIEW

Congratulations for completing the exercises that help you get the guts to be courageous and brave as you venture into entrepreneurship. The goal of this challenge is recognize that entrepreneurship is for the brave. It takes courage to transition into entrepreneurship. To find and build that courage, we need to practice being courageous in our everyday lives. Being courageous is a continual process throughout your journey into entrepreneurship.

How do you feel having completed the exercises in the first challenge? Do you feel more courageous? Do you like how you feel? Are you comfortable or uncomfortable? Describe your feelings. Remember, all feelings are valid and important.

_____

_____

_____

What feels different or is different now? For example, once I began practicing being courageous in my everyday life, I began to see that I had many ideas about starting a business. I saw myself as being much more creative than I imagined.

_____

_____

_____

Do you feel yourself moving into new territory, into the unknown? Describe that. Becoming more courageous and brave was both scary and exciting for me. I felt a lot of mixed emotions as I began to get the guts and to know myself more.

_____

_____

_____

What has this challenge stimulated in you? For example, did this challenge help you act and feel brave? Do you feel more courageous? I experienced glimpses of what my life could be like as an entrepreneur and became willing to grow.

_____

_____

Even though building courage and confidence is a continual process, you need to reward yourself for the progress you made thus far. How will you reward yourself for completing this challenge?

_____

_____

> **What you can do, or dream you can, begin it.**
> **Boldness has genius, power and magic in it.**
>
> **Johann Wolfgang Von Goethe**

CHALLENGE II
CONNECTING TO YOUR PASSION

I feel like I connect to the deepest part of myself through my quiet time and through nature. It's as if nature speaks to me – guides me and provides me with direction.

Connecting with our passion is the discovery of our aliveness and ourselves. It is the deepest and most profound connection we can experience in our lives. When we feel passion, we are enthusiastic and energetic. Passion motivates and guides us if we let it. Passion invokes many thoughts that are positive and pleasing.

How do we come to find and connect with our passion? When we think of passion, typically we connect it to being sexual. That's a good place to start because we know and understand the feelings and thoughts that are involved in feeling sexually passionate. We are totally immersed in the experience and usually feel feelings and emotions that contribute to feeling alive. This same experience – being totally immersed in the experience – exists when we connect to our passion for living and our everyday lives.

The experience of connecting with our passion expands beyond sexual aspects of our lives and into our entire life – being totally immersed in a hobby, watching your child play or smile, or enjoying your work. When we feel passionate about our everyday lives, we experience pleasure, fulfillment and satisfaction in everything we do.

Listen to your passion – nothing is more important. Passion can get you through just about any situation and give you the self-confidence you need.

Anonymous

Connecting to the Calling

*I feel like I am experiencing a calling to do something more –
something different – but I don't know what it is yet.*

Connecting to the calling allows you to experience your passion.
I met a man who started a business but ran out of money and
returned to a corporate job. About eight months later, he called to
say that the desire to be an entrepreneur just wouldn't let him go.
So this time he had a new idea and entered the new business with
money from investors. He talked about his "calling" to be an
entrepreneur. He became aware of a need to connect to the
calling so that he could become an entrepreneur. We talked about
how connecting to the calling is the connection to passion.

Becoming an entrepreneur requires an incredible amount
of passion. We need to connect to this passion – this calling – in
order to transition into entrepreneurship. This step on the path is
really quite simple; it is recognizing that you have a passion for
something greater than what you are experiencing. It is
acknowledging and connecting with your passion – that part of
you that wants to express itself. You may have always had a
calling to be a poet, an artist, or a retail storeowner. Or you may
not know what it is you would like to do; just that you want to do
something other than what you are doing. The clarity may be
buried underneath other issues and you can't see it yet, it's just a
feeling. More will be revealed; you do not need to know the
entire path or journey right now. The goal here is to simply
connect to the calling.

This calling may surface when you feel specific emotions.
I worked with a client whose passion came through frustration.
He came in for counseling because of the frustration he was
experiencing in growing his business. We worked together for
several months developing new marketing strategies and helping
him pave a way for his business progress. I saw more frustration
than happiness in his business pursuit. After several months of
seeing him experience the same frustration, I asked him, "What

do you really want to be doing?" He responded immediately: "I want to live and work in Spain." He said that for six years he'd wanted to live this dream, but was too afraid. He lived at home and was held back by his fears and his family's fears for him.

We spent the rest of the session creating tools he could use to help him connect with his passion and live his dream. We discussed meditation, positive thinking, affirmations and prayer.

About two months after this meeting, he came back for another appointment. He shared that he was going to Spain. He booked his airline tickets and had ten interviews lined up when he got there. He planned to get a job to acclimate himself before becoming self-employed again. It took him six years to acknowledge what he wanted to do and three months to connect to his passion and start doing it.

Say yes to your calling! Allow it to come forth. You may feel resistance; expect it. You may feel fear; feel it. Your feelings are important and valid. The emotions you have are normal; they have served in keeping this part of you quiet. The man who moved overseas didn't think it was possible, but once he acknowledged his calling, things began to work for him. Acknowledging your calling doesn't mean that you need to change everything overnight. It simply means you take the first step on the path and claim that part of you that allows the journey to begin.

What are you being called to do? What is your yearning? What do you really want to be doing that you are not doing?

_____

_____

_____

_____

If you do not know what your yearning is, write what this yearning feels like. If you are not sure, then describe how you would like to feel. Where is this desire coming from, what is it connected to? What do you want to feel that you are not feeling? Write about this as much as you need to. This is a good time to use your journal to let your feelings out. When you acknowledge your feelings, you acknowledge your calling – even if you do not know yet what your calling is. Write down the feelings that you want to feel.

_____

_____

_____

_____

_____

_____

How long have you had this desire? These feelings? Write about it. Remember, your feelings are valid.

_____

_____

_____

_____

_____

_____

What has been stopping you from putting this yearning into action? Connect with whatever has been stopping you. When you connect with what is stopping you, you connect to the calling. Write down why you are not doing what you would like to be doing. Remember, you are not alone.

_____

_____

_____

_____

_____

_____

I acknowledge and accept all of me.

Listen to Your Passion

I have to pay attention now to what I want, not just what I think will look good on a resume or to some other employer. When I take the focus off what I think I should do and just sit back and listen to myself, it is as if a new person is being born.

When we begin to listen, really listen to ourselves, we will discover what it is we really want to do. We will deepen our connection with ourselves and discover more of who we are and what we desire in our lives. When we listen to ourselves, we connect with ourselves.

43

Listening to ourselves requires that we stay in today and not in the future. If we are living in the future, we are not listening to ourselves and we are missing out on opportunities to connect with our passion. Sometimes we don't want to listen. I spent two years working toward a social work degree and all the while I was looking at ads in the paper for the kind of jobs I would be interested in when I got the degree. I spent hours looking at ads way before I even finished school. I forgot to stay in the day. I realized after finishing a 400-hour internship in the last semester of school that I did not want to work in the field of social work. All that time I spent looking for jobs was wasted.

Do you enjoy each day or do you try to get your days over with? One way to know if you stay in the day is to see if you enjoy each day. If you are just trying to get to the end of each day or each week – waiting for 5 p.m. or for Friday – that is a pretty good indicator that you have an opportunity to listen and connect to yourself. Describe if you stay in your day and what that experience is for you.

_____

_____

_____

_____

When you enjoy and experience each day, you can listen to your passion. When do you feel connected to life? Is it when you are playing a sport? Enjoying the outdoors? Reading a book? Learning a new skill? Write down the ways you connect with life.

1. _____

2. _____

3. _____

4. _____

5. _____

6. _____

7. _____

8. _____

9. _____

10. _____

I enjoy each day and listen to my passions.

Express Your Passion

I love to give presentations. I feel this deep sense of self-expression when I am in front of a group of people sharing my knowledge and experience.

It is important – particularly once you are aware and have acknowledged your passions – that you experience this connection regularly and get used to being in a pleasurable state for longer and regular periods of time. This is called the expression of your passion. It is one thing to know what you are passionate about; it is another to actually do it.

One of my passions is working with small business owners to help them develop their entrepreneurial skills. One of the ways I enjoy expressing my passion of working with small business owners is through professional speaking. Once I start speaking to my audience, I feel transformed. The message I deliver "becomes me" and I am completely absorbed in the moment.

In what ways will you express your passion? Will you go on hikes and day walks because you love nature and bird watching? Will you go out to dinner with friends because you enjoy socializing?

_____

_____

_____

_____

How often do you experience this connection with your passion – with what you really like to do? Daily? Weekly? Monthly? It is important to experience your passion on a regular basis in your entrepreneurial journey. I used to go days before I would take the time to connect with something I really enjoyed. Now, it is important for me to experience this connection daily.

_____

_____

_____

_____

I express my life passion in all that I do.

Acknowledge Your Strengths

I realize now that when I acknowledge my strengths I strengthen my relationship with myself. How I wish I started this sooner.

When we acknowledge our strengths we acknowledge and connect with our passion. Our strengths are what we are naturally good at. We may have great communication skills, organizational skills or writing skills. We may have a gift that we have not yet fully explored but know we want to do. I wanted to write a book for years. In looking back, I did not write or even attempt to write the book because I had not yet acknowledged that writing was one of my strengths. It wasn't until I wrote nationally recognized award nomination packages that I realized and acknowledged that writing was one of my strengths.

What are you really good at? While we each have innate abilities to help us in this world, we need to know what they are and be aware of how we use them. Strengths are part of our passion. They are what we build upon and work with in entrepreneurship. It is important for us to connect to our passion through our strengths. Write down what you are really good at or what you believe that you would be good at if you tried.

1. _____

2. _____

3. _____

4. _____

5. _____

6. _____

7. _____

8. _____

9. _____

10. _____

Look over the list you created. How many of the strengths that you listed do you connect with on a regular basis? For example, if you wrote that painting is a strength, when is the last time you painted? Yesterday? Last week? Last year? If you want to connect with your passion, connect through your strengths on a regular basis.

I acknowledge and connect with my strengths.

Develop Your Second Nature

I've worked long and hard on becoming more self-assured and now I am. I can feel it and see it in how I relate to people, how I express myself.

Our second nature is a set of attributes or strengths that are learned and practiced so much that they become part of who we are. They are our learned strengths. Our learned strengths are important because like our natural strengths, they connect us to our passion. Developing a second nature is challenging. It requires patience with ourselves as we work at developing these new attributes and periodically fall back in our old, familiar ways. It also requires the ability to avoid stressful situations and overextend ourselves, both of which will return us to what is familiar – the old habits we're working to avoid. Taking good care of ourselves emotionally, mentally, physically and spiritually is important to maintain the effectiveness of our second nature.

The first step to developing a second nature is to have the desire to further connect with our passion, not necessarily the desire to eliminate the behavior that bothers us. I have seen clients develop their learned strengths for the sake of their business. Interestingly, if we help our business, we help ourselves. Usually, we will not do things differently in our lives just for the sake of trying something new.

Take Mary, for example. She came in for business counseling because she felt dissatisfied with her small gift shop that was not growing. While she had the desire to grow a flourishing business, she shared that she did not have the natural ability to be organized or handle finances. She realized that her lack of these abilities was negatively impacting her business because she spent so much time trying to keep up with her disorganization. For years, she avoided her financial situation by paying bills late, spending a lot of time and energy looking for bills, calling collectors back, paying late fees and driving to drop off checks to companies she owed money to. Her inability to deal with her finances was limiting her ability to connect with and experience her passion – growing a successful business.

To develop her second nature of effectively dealing with her finances, she created a daily task list. She also organized her desk and put all her bills in one place, she set up accounting software on her computer and paid her bills weekly. She also met with her accountant and set up a budget. Slowly, her organizational and financial skills become her learned strengths – her second nature.

Her payoff for developing her second nature, the ability to be organized, was that she began to deepen her connection with her passion and see clearly what she really wanted to be doing – operating a boutique gift shop in a high-end location. Within three months of developing her second nature, Mary was able to get out of the two-year lease on her small store and relocate to a store twice the size and in an area of town where she wanted to be. Her second nature helped her connect with her passion.

What strengths do you need that you do not naturally have? For example, do you need to learn to save money or become comfortable talking with people you do not know?

1. _____

2. _____

3. _____

4. _____

5. _____

How will you develop each of those learned strengths or abilities? Will you open a savings account and commit to saving a certain amount each month? Will you begin going to networking meetings and begin talking with people you do not know?

1. _____

2. _____

3. _____

4. _____

5. _____

Your second nature will become natural strengths as long as two requirements are met: First, that you practice your learned strengths on a regular basis, and second, that you maintain a balanced lifestyle. In what ways do you need to balance your life (i.e. avoid high stress, get enough rest, etc.) while you work at developing and maintaining your second nature?

_____

_____

_____

_____

_____

| *I continually develop and strengthen my second nature.* |

Like and Accept Yourself

I can say with conviction that I love my life and me – I really do – I accept all of me.

Self-acceptance is total acceptance of who you are and where you are in your life. Whatever your life circumstances, acceptance can help you connect with your passion. Acceptance doesn't mean that you like every circumstance in your life. Acceptance simply is saying and believing, "I accept where I am in my life today." That's it. Acceptance is acceptance. When we accept ourselves, we accept our passion. It is when we fight acceptance that we disconnect from our passion and are challenged to move forward. Practicing acceptance brings about a new energy to help us stay connected to who we are and what we want to be doing.

It wasn't until I accepted myself for being afraid and needing assistance (spiritually and emotionally) in making the transition into entrepreneurship that I was able to connect with my passion. Why? Because when I was fighting acceptance I was fighting myself. Acceptance helps us connect and stay connected.

What do you like and accept about yourself? Do you like that you have a great personality? Get along with others easily? Are organized and focused?

_____

_____

_____

What don't you want to accept about yourself? For example, I had a hard time accepting that I felt uncomfortable in social situations. I didn't like accepting that I had panic attacks when I was in public. When I began to accept all of me – panic attacks, discomfort and all – I began to move through these experiences and deepen my connection with myself. I haven't had a panic attack in years and am now comfortable in most social situations. Write down what you don't want to accept about yourself. You may want to use your journal for this exercise.

_____

_____

_____

_____

What work do you need to do now that you admitted that you don't want to accept a part of yourself? (This answer may not come to you right away. Come back to this question in a day or two if necessary.) In the example above, when I began to accept all of me, I found it necessary to work with a professional counselor to help deal with these challenges. While professional counseling is not always necessary, it is helpful if we cannot move through experiences by ourselves.

_____

_____

_____

Write a note to yourself about accepting all of you – the parts of yourself that you like and the parts of yourself that you do not like or don't want to accept. (This is important. Expect to feel resistance and other emotions. Do this exercise even if you don't want to or don't feel like it and feel your feelings.)

Dear _____,

_____

_____

_____

_____

_____

_____

_____

I like and accept all of me.

Connect with Nature

Nature and natural places center me and connect me to me.

When we connect with nature we connect with ourselves. When I was trying to leave my job the first time, I would spend my lunch hour wondering through a nature trail and simply connecting with nature. Nature soothes and guides us if we let it.

What I have learned about myself is that the more I get to know, nurture and love myself, the more time I need to spend in nature. Going for nature walks, exploring state parks, swimming in springs, lakes and oceans, hiking, camping – it's all part of connecting with myself through nature.

Nature is everywhere, we just need to look for it and then immerse ourselves in it. We can enjoy the flowers in our garden, the fruit on the trees, the birds that sing in the morning, the sound of the wind, the beauty in the sky.

In what ways to you enjoy nature? Do you enjoy fishing in the ocean? Swimming in a lake? Walking on the beach? Hiking in a forest? Gazing at stars? List at least ten ways you enjoy nature.

1. _____

2. _____

3. _____

4. _____

5. _____

6. _____

7. _____

8. _____

9. _____

10. _____

Seek out nature, connect with it and find yourself in it.

Enjoy Simple Pleasures

*I notice that the little things are what really matter. The more I
pay attention to life's simple pleasures, the more I find pleasure
in my life.*

Simple pleasures are seconds or moments that we connect with
something or someone through enjoyment. For me, this means
enjoying something outside of myself such as seeing a newborn
baby, seeing children laugh or enjoying the stillness in the night.
The old saying, "stop and smell the roses" means enjoy simple
pleasures.

Simple pleasures are very important. They help us stay
connected to our passion and purpose in life. They help us
appreciate ourselves and our lives. In this age of automation and
complexity, we may have to look more closely at our lives and
our surroundings to enjoy simple pleasures and stay connected to
our passion.

What simple pleasures did you enjoy today? Become consciously
aware of moments when you simply felt enjoyment and
appreciation. It could be watching your child play, listening to
raindrops, or enjoying a delicious meal.

Simple pleasures you enjoyed:

Day 1: _____

_____

_____

Day 2: _____

_____

_____

Day 3: _____

_____

_____

Day 4: _____

_____

_____

Day 5: _____

_____

_____

Day 6: _____

_____

_____

Day 7: _____

_____

_____

> **_I am aware of and enjoy simple pleasures._**

Connect with Your Hobbies, Play and Have Fun!

I love to do so many things...camping, bike riding, kayaking,
scuba diving, skiing. The more I take the time to enjoy my
hobbies, the more connected I feel to life.

An important part of connecting with our passion is through play, hobbies and fun. Hobbies feed, nourish and re-energize us. A lawyer who writes novels in his spare time has the hobby of writing. Perhaps he is a better lawyer because of his connection with his hobby.

Play allows us to be creative, to shift from structure and order to creativity and fun. Play can be a walk on the beach, a game of tennis, a bike ride, a dance or any form of healthy fun that you enjoy.

What are your hobbies? Do you like to swim? Dance? In what ways do you play and have fun?

1. _____

2. _____

3. _____

4. _____

5. _____

If you do not have any hobbies, what hobbies would you like to pursue? Is there any hobby from your past that you did or wanted to do that you might consider adding to your life today?

_____

_____

_____

_____

Part of becoming more aware of our connection with our passion is becoming aware of how we spend our time and how we feel. I've seen people who feel stress and anxiety and don't know why. By consciously choosing to be committed to our hobbies and to play, we are consciously choosing to stay connected to our passion.

What is your commitment to your hobbies, play and fun? Will you play tennis once a week? Join a softball league? Take up fencing? Start bicycling?

_____

_____

_____

_____

_____

I enjoy my hobbies.

Feel Your Feelings

I never used to like to feel my feelings, especially the uncomfortable ones. Now I know that feeling my feelings is a way of connecting to myself and to my passion. The more I feel and connect with my feelings, the more entrepreneurial I become.

Too often we stop feeling and spend most of our time doing. When this happens, we disconnect from ourselves. It is in this disconnection that we "forget" and stop doing what we like and love. If we don't feel our feelings, then we don't experience the connection to our lives. We need to learn to feel all our feelings to stay connected to our passion – to ourselves.

One of the ways I feel my feelings is to write them down. Since my first instinct is to do rather than feel, I have had to learn to stop long enough to recognize what I am feeling. I can get so caught up in my day that I do not feel my feelings. If I am not careful, I can spend a whole day and not recognize a single feeling. When I catch myself doing that, I start writing. What am I feeling in this moment? Am I tired? Hungry? Happy? Bored? Serene?

Feeling feelings can be exhausting at first but we can get in the habit of feeling our feelings. On several occasions, I have used the following exercise to remind myself to feel. For one day, write down what you are feeling every thirty minutes. In order to connect with a feeling or feel a feeling, you may need to take a moment to be still and quiet to allow a feeling to surface. Once you feel a feeling, whatever it may be, write it down. Expect to feel resistance if you have never completed an exercise like this before. By acknowledging your feelings and writing them down, you connect with yourself – with your passion. Return to this exercise anytime you disconnect from your feelings and from your passion.

6:00 a.m.	
6:30 a.m.	
7:00 a.m.	
7:30 a.m.	
8:00 a.m.	
8:30 a.m.	
9:00 a.m.	
9:30 a.m.	
10:00 a.m.	
10:30 a.m.	
11:00 a.m.	
11:30 a.m.	
12:00 noon	
12:30 p.m.	
1:00 p.m.	
1:30 p.m.	
2:00 p.m.	
2:30 p.m.	
3:00 p.m.	
3:30 p.m.	
4:00 p.m.	
4:30 p.m.	
5:00 p.m.	
5:30 p.m.	
6:00 p.m.	
6:30 p.m.	
7:00 p.m.	
7:30 p.m.	
8:00 p.m.	
8:30 p.m.	
9:00 p.m.	
9:30 p.m.	
10:00 p.m.	

I feel all my feelings.

Get Honest with Yourself

One of my goals this year is to really get honest with myself and do what feels "right."

The way to totally expand our connection with ourselves is to be completely honest with ourselves. Total honesty is how we connect with our passion and our truth. We can disconnect from who we really are, from what we really want in life, because we lack self-honesty. We stop listening to ourselves and begin to believe our own lies.

My friend Gina realized that she was not being honest with herself. She called me crying about a work situation and came over to my house. After several hours of talking about her job and the situation that upset her, she realized that what was really bothering her was that she was not doing what she wanted to be doing professionally.

She had been working as a bookkeeper for years and knew, deep in her heart, that she wanted to be an artist. Even though she was good at being a bookkeeper, she was not satisfied with her work. Sometimes being good at something can confuse us into thinking we like doing it. Gina is an artist and she wants to paint for a living. When she paints, she is fulfilled. Her ability to listen to herself and get honest with herself helped her believe her truth, that she can be an artist rather than believe her lies that tell her she can't make a living without a bookkeeping job.

It is common to come to a level of self-honesty through pain or discomfort. Sometimes, our painful situations get our attention and motivate us to get honest with ourselves. Pain is a great motivator for honesty.

Practice self-honesty. Listen to yourself and allow your truth to be revealed. It's OK. Take baby steps in practicing self-honesty. It is vital to your long-term connection to your passion. Many of us denied our truths and lost our connection. We tried living according to what our bosses or family members wanted from us, telling ourselves it was what we wanted, too. It is time for us to be our own cheerleaders, to listen to ourselves, believe in ourselves and get totally honest with who we are and what we want. As we learn to live in total honesty, we can be empowered and totally connected to who we are. This level of honesty is where we find our true selves, our passion and our power.

Write your statement of self-dishonesty, specifically the way or ways you are not being honest with yourself. Then write your statement of self-honesty and your commitment to self-honesty. For example, are you honest with yourself about your job? Do you like what you do? Are you doing your job because you want to be doing it or because you are afraid to do something different? It is by recognizing dishonesty that we can commit to self-honesty.

Example:

Statement of self-dishonesty:

I don't know what I want to do so I am better off staying at this job until I know.

Statement of self-honesty:

I am afraid to make a change in my job situation.

Commitment to self-honesty:

I am willing to start exploring other options by listing priorities in my life right now.

Statement of self-dishonesty:

_____

_____

Statement of self-honesty:

_____

_____

Commitment to self-honesty:

_____

_____

Statement of self-dishonesty:

_____

_____

Statement of self-honesty:

_____

_____

Commitment to self-honesty:

_____

_____

Statement of self-dishonesty:

_____

_____

Statement of self-honesty:

_____

_____

Commitment to self-honesty:

_____

_____

| *I am honest with myself.* |

Take Care of Old Business

*I feel like I'm constantly moving out of the old
and into the new.*

Old business can interfere with new business. Old business can be anything that gets in the way of listening to ourselves and connecting us to our passion. Old business actually keeps us right where we are until we address it and resolve it. Old business can be a bill you've resisted paying, a pile of clothes that you've been meaning to take to the thrift store, a leak in your washing machine that simply annoys you, or a relationship that is not working in your best interest that you continually return to.

What old business, things or situations do you need to take care of? Even if you don't want to take care of them, just write them down. If you cannot think of anything, think of what annoys or bothers you that you just don't seem to take care of. This "old business" may present itself over time. Do not be in a hurry to write them all down at this moment, you can return to this exercise at any time.

1. _____

2. _____

3. _____

4. _____

5. _____

6. _____

7. _____

8. _____

9. _____

10. _____

Your list may be long or short; that is not important. What is important is that you get your old business written down on paper, and then begin to resolve your old business, one thing at a time. The first time I became aware of all the old business in my life, the list was long. The issues built up over the years until I began to address and resolve them one by one. My yard had too many weeds, my kitchen appliances needed to be replaced, my shower leaked water into the garage, etc. As I began to take care of one area, the next and then the next, I felt better about my ability to accomplish things I didn't want to do and it freed my mind to listen to my passion. I still have things on my list, but I know they are there; I've recognized them and am constantly working on them, rather than waiting years for them to accumulate again.

Prioritize the list and make a commitment of when you will take care of each item.

What you need to do	**Start date**
1. _____	_____
2. _____	_____
3. _____	_____
4. _____	_____
5. _____	_____
6. _____	_____
7. _____	_____
8. _____	_____
9. _____	_____
10. _____	_____

I take care of old business.

Let Go of Regrets

What good does it do to regret something that is now only a piece of history? It can't be changed anyway. It's time to let go of the past, live in today and start planning for my future.

As odd as it might sound, this phase of connecting with your passion is also about letting go of old behavior, the things that no longer work for us but that we continue to hold onto. When we let go of regrets, we deepen our connection with ourselves. Letting go of regrets is about moving on, letting go of what was or wasn't – whether it was right or wrong. Regrets keep us disconnected and hold us back. Since our goal is to move forward, we ultimately must choose to let go of what isn't working to make room for what can.

What regrets do you have? Do you regret not starting a business sooner? Do you regret passing up an opportunity to move to a different state ten years ago? Do you regret not going away to college or finishing school?

1. _____

2. _____

3. _____

4. _____

5. _____

6. _____

7. _____

8. _____

9. _____

10. _____

In what ways do these regrets hold you back? Do you still think about how you could have done things differently? How much time and energy do you put into thinking about situations from the past?

_____

_____

_____

_____

_____

_____

Describe your regrets. List what action will replace an old regret. What will you do to modify that behavior or old way of thinking?

Example:

Regret/Grudge:

I am still angry about how David treated me.

New Action to replace the Regret/Grudge:

I forgive David. I am replacing my thoughts of anger toward him with thoughts of kindness.

Regret/Grudge:

_____

_____

New Action to replace the Regret/Grudge:

_____

_____

Regret/Grudge:

_____

_____

New Action to replace the Regret/Grudge:

_____

_____

Regret/Grudge:

_____

_____

New Action to replace the Regret/Grudge:

_____

_____

I move forward when I forgive.

CONNECTING TO YOUR PASSION CHALLENGE REVIEW

As we allow ourselves to come forth, to connect with our passion, we come to experience more of who we are. When we do that, we discover our true entrepreneurial calling. We feel our feelings, get to know ourselves and experience the connection with our passion and with ourselves. In this challenge, we discover our enthusiasm by listening to ourselves and connecting to our passion. We get honest with ourselves and take responsibility for our actions. We let go of the past by taking care of old business and creating peace with our past. We learn that in letting go of the past, we are ready for our future. We connect with our passion and our enthusiasm so that we can transition into our entrepreneurial lifestyle.

In what ways are you experiencing a greater connection with yourself and your passion? For example, are you beginning to enjoy and pay attention to simple pleasures? Are you taking time to connect with nature?

_____

_____

_____

_____

_____

_____

_____

What did you learn about yourself or bring back to life within yourself? For example, are you experiencing a new freedom from letting go of a regret or getting honest with yourself?

_____

_____

_____

_____

_____

In what ways do you feel inspired to continue connecting with your passion?

_____

_____

_____

> **A man can succeed at almost anything for which he has unlimited enthusiasm.**
>
> **Charles Schwab**

CHALLENGE III
PREPARING YOUR MIND, BODY AND SPIRIT

I realize that I experienced an incredible amount of personal and professional growth the past year. I made a lot of changes. I feel like I blossomed. I expanded – in knowledge, in life, in experience, in love.

Preparing the mind, body and spirit for entrepreneurship is like preparing the mind, body and spirit for the Olympics. We change and improve ourselves. Preparing for entrepreneurship requires similar changes – a preparation that is beyond our normal, everyday lives. Just like the Olympic trainer knows he or she will need to train differently to move into a greater level of competition, so it is with us. We need to prepare ourselves by making changes to win this race against ourselves, to outrace old patterns and ways of thinking and living, to move beyond what we have known and done in the past.

Things do not change, we change.

Henry David Thoreau

Examine Your Beliefs

I need to go back – way back – to seek out my old beliefs and rewrite them so they work for me instead of against me.

Beliefs are what we believe about our circumstances or ourselves. Beliefs are typically unconscious thoughts that lay the foundation for our lives. They are the basis for how we live, how we act and how we function in the world. Beliefs can work for us or against us. Often, we do not recognize which beliefs work against us until an issue arises where we see a pattern and begin to ask ourselves what belief we have that consistently brings a particular circumstance into our lives. For example, sometimes people have a belief that life is really very difficult and so they unconsciously create situations that reinforce that belief. Our beliefs can affect our personal and professional lives. That same belief of thinking that life is difficult may translate in our professional lives to attracting clients who won't pay us or who mistreat us. How we are treated can often be reflected in what we believe we deserve or how we believe we should be treated.

Examining beliefs, seeing what they are and changing them, if necessary – is essential for a healthy life and entrepreneurial journey. Many clients have old beliefs that need to be changed. Often, these beliefs are about money. Old beliefs about money can seriously affect a business without your even being aware of how they impact you.

You may have always heard from your parents that a desire for money meant you were greedy or bad. Rosemary grew up believing that having money was bad. Some of the messages she shared after reflecting on this issue and writing down her thoughts were, "Money leads to evil," "Rich people lie," "Money will make me greedy." Rosemary had a difficult time recognizing her beliefs because they were the only beliefs about money that she had ever known. She never thought of challenging them or evaluating them because they were part of her.

So, how do you get in touch with your beliefs? The first step is to write down thoughts and reflect on areas that seem to be patterns in your life. Mike did this exercise and saw that he had a lot of trouble with his beliefs about money. He didn't understand why he continually had financial struggles. He was intelligent and a smart businessman but he wasn't able to make a living without struggling. He began to ask himself why he had these challenges. What was the problem? Why couldn't he seem to move beyond these challenges? Soon he discovered the root of his financial challenge – his beliefs. He realized that he grew up with negative messages about money. These negative beliefs about money affected his ability to enjoy a prosperous life and caused him to live with constant financial struggles.

Know that your old beliefs may not come to you automatically. Sometimes an old belief will come to your consciousness when you see that you have repeated a pattern or a behavior that you did not want to repeat. It is at this time that you can stimulate it to consciousness and then decide if that particular belief serves you or not.

This experience of identifying your beliefs can bring up many feelings. Feeling your feelings is an important part of this exercise. When you feel your feelings, especially uncomfortable ones, you are identifying your beliefs. It is when we can identify them that we can choose to change them. The following steps will help you raise your beliefs to a conscious level and identify them. You may want to use your journal to write down your experiences.

1. Practice slowing down and experiencing quiet time. The goal of quiet time is to "be" rather than "do." One idea is to take the time to slow down and enjoy your surroundings – enjoy the sunrise, the sound of the ocean, birds soaring, the beauty of nature. Practice slowing down and experiencing quiet time several times throughout the day on a regular basis. This exercise is not only important for beliefs to surface but is important to maintain a desirable level of living.

2. After you enjoy quiet time, ask your beliefs to be revealed to you. Ask yourself, "What do I believe about myself and my life?" "What beliefs do I have that are helping me or hindering my progress?" "What beliefs result in me repeating patterns that I do not want to repeat?" Ask yourself other questions unique to you. Write down the thoughts that come to you. Let your thoughts flow. Allow yourself to feel whatever feelings

surface along with your beliefs. Expect to feel feelings while you do this exercise. Sometimes painful feelings and memories will surface during this part of the exercise.

3.   Look for situations in your past that have memories attached to them. What did your mother or father use to say to you as a child that you now believe about yourself, your circumstances, or your life? My mother told me that children should be seen and not heard. So for many years, in my personal and professional life, I didn't have a "voice," per se. I didn't think that what I had to say was important. I changed this belief to "My voice is valuable and I am worthy to be listened to and heard."

Repeat these steps as often as necessary until you feel that you can identify what your beliefs are. Once you feel that you have raised your beliefs to a conscious level, proceed to the next section. I have worked with many clients who realized that their entire set of beliefs, or belief system, came from others – mostly family members. Know that the beliefs revealed to you may not be yours. They may only be what you were taught and ultimately believed. These old beliefs have made people believe they are lazy, not worthy, not smart, not capable, and the list goes on. We have the power and ability to change our old beliefs.

Write your old beliefs and your new beliefs about money. Your old belief is the belief that you either learned or were raised to believe. Your new belief is what you are aspiring to believe.

Old Belief: _____

New Belief: _____

Old Belief: _____

New Belief: _____

Old Belief: _____

New Belief: _____

Write your beliefs about success and failure. What does success mean to you? What does failure mean to you? Does success mean having security? That is what Gina believed. Gina's mother told her that having security was important in life. Security meant getting a good job that would provide health insurance. When Gina was in her twenties, she acted on her mother's belief system. She got a job with health insurance so she would feel secure and thus be successful. The problem was that Gina didn't feel successful, even though she had her mother's sense of security. She challenged this belief about security because she realized that no job was secure. Gina changed her belief of what security and success meant. For her, security and success is being her own boss. She left her job and started a business while in her early thirties, and bought her own health insurance.

Old Belief: _____

New Belief: _____

Old Belief: _____

New Belief: _____

Old Belief: _____

New Belief: _____

Write your old beliefs about yourself and the new beliefs that you choose to replace your old beliefs with. This can be a tough exercise because you are challenging your core beliefs – you are challenging yourself. Is who you are what you believe? John believed that he was lazy and not worthy to have what he desired. He believed this at 40 years of age because it was what his mother used to tell him when he was a child. He completed all of the schooling to become a chiropractor and yet he believed he was lazy. His belief about not being worthy showed up in his inability to transition into being a full-time chiropractor. He worked 40 hours a week repairing golf carts – a job that was a far cry from being a chiropractor. John's belief about being lazy affected his ability to move into the career he desired. He realized after doing this exercise that his belief about being lazy and not being worthy was an old belief and was not valid in his life as an adult. He replaced this belief with his truth, a belief that he enjoyed working hard on projects that he enjoyed and that he was a good chiropractor. Since changing his beliefs, John bought a chiropractor practice.

Old Belief: _____

New Belief: _____

Old Belief: _____

New Belief: _____

Old Belief: _____

New Belief: _____

Your new beliefs play a vital role in moving you forward in your personal and entrepreneurial efforts. They are similar to affirmations in that you may not believe them yet but you know they are or will be true for you. Transfer your new beliefs on index cards and read them daily or put them somewhere where they will be visible to you. I used to write my new beliefs on Post-It notes and put them in my desk drawer so that when I opened my drawer, I was reminded of my new beliefs.

What will you do to congratulate yourself for completing a difficult exercise? Taking time for yourself is an important part of the entrepreneurial journey. Will you enjoy spending time with friends? Enjoy time alone doing one of your favorite hobbies?

_____

_____

_____

My beliefs support me and my journey.

Think Positive!

As far as money goes, that is a bigger challenge than I thought. I never realized how powerful negative thoughts about money are. I am taking a new perspective in this area of my life – the more I have and appreciate, the more will be given to me.

Positive, life-giving, energy-enhancing thoughts need to be present with you at all times. Think positive. Positive thoughts lead to positive actions. Negative thoughts, on the other hand, delay progress and affect our ability to make positive changes in our lives. When negative thoughts creep into your mind, ask them or tell them to leave. You can no longer afford to think negatively. How can you tell if you are thinking positively or negatively? You can tell if your thoughts are positive or negative by examining them and seeing if they start with comments such as, "I will never…" or "I can't." Pay attention to your feelings.

Positive thoughts help us feel good and negative thoughts make us feel bad. For example, if you think about your business venture and feel excited and energized, than you are most likely thinking positive thoughts such as, "The business is going to do great!" "I am living the life of my dreams." If, on the other hand, you think thoughts that make you feel upset, drained or anxious, you are likely thinking negative thoughts. We may catch ourselves making "I can't" statements. Be aware that any statement that starts with "I can't" contributes to negative thinking and negative thoughts. Negative thoughts include, "I can't quit my job." "I can't make enough money if I start a business." "I will never be able to make it on my own." "I might not make enough money if I start a business."

Examine your thoughts. How do you feel about them? What are your negative thoughts? Write them down. Beneath each negative thought, write down a positive thought to replace it.

Example:

Negative thought:

I will never be able to save enough money to leave this job and start a business.

Positive thought:

I set goals, am saving money and plan to start a business while I am still employed.

Negative thought:

_____

_____

Positive thought:

_____

_____

Negative thought:

_____

_____

Positive thought:

_____

_____

Negative thought:

_____

_____

Positive thought:

_____

_____

Become willing to change. Become consciously aware of your thoughts and work at thinking positively. The goal of this exercise is to replace negative thoughts with positive ones and to retrain your mind to think positively so you can open yourself to new opportunities and experiences. Each time you have a negative thought, replace it with a positive one. That may mean saying the positive thought to yourself quietly or out loud or writing it down.

> *I think positive thoughts.*

Affirm, Affirm, Affirm. Affirmations Work.

I believe I'm going to succeed in whatever I do. I have flooded my mind, so to say, with positive affirmations.

Affirmations are important and powerful. Affirmations are positive statements that you either believe or want to believe that are stated in the present tense. For example, "I am filled with prosperity and abundance." You may feel that this statement may or may not be true – yet – however, saying and believing it helps make it a reality.

Create affirmations and read them daily. One night, I stayed up until 1 a.m. creating affirmations. I wrote them on 3x5 cards, decorated them, strung them together and hung them on my bathroom mirrors. I read them every day, every time I used the bathroom and kept them there until I believed what they said. I have since created a new set of cards. As we change, we grow and experience new levels of thinking, sometimes in ways we didn't think was possible. Affirmations help make the seemingly impossible possible. Issues that we thought we could not overcome, we overcome by changing ourselves and using affirmations. If this feels uncomfortable, start with the affirmations at the end of each exercise throughout this book – they are all designed to inspire you.

Create at least 10 affirmations for yourself. Write them in the present tense – as if the statement is already happening. For example, if you are challenged with financial security, write a statement like, "I make $85,000 a year and love my life!"

Write your affirmations below and then transfer them to 3x5 cards or wallet-size cards. Post them or have them somewhere that you can read them at least once a day. When you read them, feel the feeling that you would feel as if the affirmation were already true. For example, if your affirmation is "I am successful and prosperous," believe that you already are experiencing success and prosperity and feel the feelings.

Affirmations:

1. _____

2. _____

3. _____

4. _____

5. _____

6. _____

7. _____

8. _____

9. _____

10. _____

Read over the list of affirmations you created and say them out loud, believing what you are saying. When you say your affirmations, feel what it feels like to experience what they imply. The goal is to eventually bring the affirmations into fruition – to experience them. Do this exercise even if it feels uncomfortable or silly; it is supposed to feel different if you have never done this type of exercise before. Be willing to change. Describe how you feel having said your affirmations with belief that they are true. Did you feel empowered? Confident? After doing this exercise once a day for a week, describe any changes in thoughts or behaviors that may have resulted from creating, saying and believing your affirmations.

_____

_____

_____

_____

_____

_____

The benefit of creating and reading your affirmations on a regular basis is to create the feelings that you described above. If you created powerful affirmations, when you say and believe the affirmations, they will empower you. Affirmations will be especially helpful during the early phases of your transition into entrepreneurship – that is when most people, including myself, experience a lot of self-doubt and a tremendous amount of uncertainty.

I am capable of achieving anything I desire.

Visualize. If You See It, You Can Create It

I can see my "dream" coming true – I see it all coming together – speaking, writing, consulting – that has been my vision for several years now.

Visualization is helpful in bringing forth the outcome or experience you desire. Visualization means to practice and review desirable scenarios in your mind about your future. I have found that clients who can "see" their business and its progress have a better chance to achieve it. Their job is to manifest or bring forth the desired outcome and be open to greatness of any kind – even if it is not part of the visualization.

One of my favorite analogies with regard to practicing visualization is planning a trip. You may plan to go to Alaska. You have never been there but you begin to get excited about it and actually experience the excitement of being there. You feel what it feels like to be there and visualize what it will be like when you are actually there. This process is similar to creating visualizations for your business. Even if you do not yet know what type of business you desire to be in or start, you can visualize the feelings of success, the experience of being your own boss, and the feeling of sharing your business with others.

Gloria completed this visualization exercise as part of a business counseling session. She shared that she had never taken the time to visualize what her future would be like. She hadn't thought of what she wanted to do in 10 years or in 20 years. After completing the visualization exercise, she set an overall direction for her future. It helped her know what she was working toward.

Begin visualizing what you would like to create. Make sure when you do this exercise that you are relaxed. Take a few deep breaths and close your eyes if you'd like. How does your future look? What do you see? A company with a lot or a few employees? A one-person business? A company that provides products, services or both? What are you selling? Who are your customers? Write down what you visualize.

_____

_____

_____

What do you see a year from now? A larger company? More employees? New services?

_____

_____

_____

_____

Now, think about three years from now. What does the business look like? What amount of revenue are you making? Are you in the same office space or a larger space? How has your company grown?

_____

_____

_____

_____

Now look five years down the road. How do you visualize your business in five years? Are you preparing the business for further growth or to sell? How has your company grown?

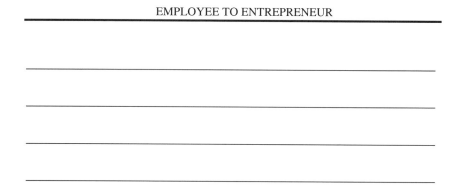

The goal of this exercise is to create a vision for you to work toward and practice seeing that vision on a regular basis. If you like, you can do this exercise with your personal life as well – looking one year, three years, five years or more into your future. The visualization exercise can serve as a guide to your future. Anytime you are not sure what you are doing or where your business is going, you can return to this exercise to help you refocus and gain a direction to work toward.

I visualize the future I desire.

Get Organized!

I spent a good part of the day working on Excel spreadsheets and balancing numbers. I also cleaned my room and organized my office. I threw away a lot, too – making room for the "new."

Getting organized is a prerequisite for mental preparation in our entrepreneurial journey. Organization helps us build balance into our lives and not waste our energy. For example, I regularly waited until my car was in dire need of gas before I would stop at a gas station. I would feel stressed and be worried because my gas tank was so low that I might just run out of gas before I could get to a gas station. I recognized that I was creating my own problem and it was completely unnecessary. Once I became aware of the opportunity to improve my organizational skills in this area, I made a commitment to get gas when I needed it and not wait until the stress prompted me to stop and get gas.

Organization starts by setting the goal that you want to be organized, deciding where to start and then making a concerted effort to change. Once you commit to being organized, areas that need to be organized will present themselves to you. For example, I made a decision that I needed to get my business organized. Once I made that decision and began the process of getting organized, I realized that I was running my business from my entire house, not just my office. I discovered that I had business cards on my nightstand, in my purse, on my kitchen counter, and on my dining room table. I saw the same pattern with business newspapers and mail.

I have to continue to work on maintaining my organizational abilities, as it is natural to fall back into old, familiar but ineffective patterns.

Take a look at how well organized your personal and professional belongings are. Go over the following organizational checklist and answer the questions below.

	Yes	**No**
Automobile		
Is your car neat and tidy?	____	____
Do you have plenty of gasoline in your car?	____	____
Do you have your car repaired in a timely manner?	____	____
Do you have your oil changed regularly?	____	____

	Yes	No

Household

Are your closets neat and tidy? _____ _____

Is your kitchen clean? _____ _____

Do you have plenty of food
in your refrigerator? _____ _____

Do you make your bed daily? _____ _____

Is your bedroom
neat and tidy? _____ _____

Business

Are you usually on time
for appointments? _____ _____

Do you schedule adequate time
between appointments? _____ _____

Do you return calls within 24-hours? _____ _____

Is your office neat and tidy? _____ _____

Can you find things quickly? _____ _____

What did you learn about yourself from this exercise? Are you more or less organized than you thought? Did you recognize that you spend time thinking about or worrying about items that need to be better organized? Is there any other area of your life that you need to organize that was not listed?

_____

_____

_____

Go back over the exercise above and write down your commitment date to improving your organizational skills for each question you answered "no" to. It has been said that it takes seven attempts to change before we break a habit. Therefore, take your time working through this exercise. I would suggest that you work on improving one item a week. The goal here is to improve our organizational skills and make long-lasting change.

I am constantly improving my organizational skills.

Keep Your Eye on the Ball - Stay Focused!

I am beginning to see that if I stay focused I can achieve what I desire.

Staying focused is usually more challenging than getting focused. Usually, we can get focused rather quickly. Anything is possible for a day. The challenge comes, however, when we need to stay focused, to decide on a particular course of action and persevere in what we are doing.

Staying focused requires commitment, determination and belief in what you are doing. Learning how to stay focused is important to the progress and growth of your venture. For example, I recognized that each time I accepted a new consulting project I had to deal with feelings of procrastination and wanting to do other work. I felt this procrastination whether the project was new and exciting or if the project was difficult. Any project that was new to me brought challenges of staying focused.

Setting deadlines work well to help me stay focused. I break down a project into smaller tasks and commit myself to achieving each task. I also let my client know when they can expect the completion of a particular project.

How do you stay focused? Do you take small breaks in your workday? Do you have a task list that you work from? List at least five steps that you use or will use to stay focused.

1. _____

2. _____

3. _____

4. _____

5. _____

Focus + Priorities + Balance = Amazing Progress

Practice Self-Discipline

If we do what we always did, we will get what we always got.
I have to remind myself of this from time to time.

Making changes and sticking to them comes easier for some of us than for others. Regardless, self-discipline, which is a behavior we can learn, is necessary to support new ways of thinking and living.

When I left my job for the third time, I knew that I needed to change some of my behaviors and practice self-discipline to stay on the path I created. Otherwise I would slip back into my fears and return to my old job again. I began a daily routine that included prayer and meditation, reading affirmations and writing in my journal. To give myself an extra boost or dose of self-discipline, I bought a book by Iyanla Vanzant called "One Day My Soul Just Opened Up" (Simon and Schuster, 1998) and each day, both morning and night, for the first forty days of the new year, I disciplined myself to do the exercises in the book. I was willing to change and my self-discipline was a reflection of my willingness.

Lisa wanted to change. She knew how self-discipline could help her change but was not yet willing to commit to it. So what happens when she didn't commit herself to self-discipline? Because she had not been disciplined for long enough to have the benefits of change, she continually slipped back to what she knew – confusion and lack of focus.

Self-discipline requires a commitment to ourselves. If we want to experience our lives in a new way, we have to be willing to discipline ourselves in ways that support what we are trying to achieve. Self-discipline works – but we have to be willing to commit ourselves to practicing these behaviors on a regular basis.

Consider the progress you are working toward achieving, and then examine your daily, weekly and monthly habits. See if your habits are aligned with what you are trying to achieve. Do your habits reflect self-discipline or lack of self-discipline? For example, if your habit is to watch several hours of television per night, ask yourself, "Is this habit contributing or deterring my progress?" If the answer is that it is deterring your progress, then decide how you can be disciplined with the television. Perhaps you can limit the number of hours you watch it or decide not to watch it on certain evenings.

List your habits. What habits are comfortable and familiar to you?

1. _____

2. _____

3. _____

4. _____

5. _____

6. _____

7. _____

8. _____

9. _____

10. _____

Look over these habits and decide if they are contributing to your progress or deterring you from progress. Then decide which habits to keep, which to change and which to discontinue. Add new habits that would benefit your progress such as what has been suggested throughout this book – enjoying simple pleasures, having fun, journaling, etc., and then list the habits you are committed to on a daily, weekly, monthly basis.

Daily habits

1. _____

2. _____

3. _____

4. _____

5. _____

Weekly habits

1. _____

2. _____

3. _____

4. _____

5. _____

Monthly habits

1. _____

2. _____

3. _____

4. _____

5. _____

I am committed to my personal and professional progress.

Meditation is a Business Tool

I really had an incredible meditation this evening. It was like something I had never experienced before. My body was totally relaxed, my eyes were closed and my breathing was slow. I really enjoyed it. Usually, I'm rushing to get it over with – like it is a chore – but I actually found it enjoyable.

According to Webster's Dictionary, meditation is continued or extended thought; contemplation or spiritual introspection. It is my experience and the experience of many of my clients that meditation served to help us make changes in our lives. It helped us transition into entrepreneurship. It helps ease worries, and it helps us feel a deep sense of purpose in what we are working to achieve. Meditation is a powerful spiritual tool that can often help us in ways we cannot completely comprehend.

The best way to start a meditation routine is to simply start. Meditation on a consistent basis will help clear your mind, slow you down, and move you beyond your prior limits. If you have never meditated, you can expect to feel resistance in developing a meditation routine.

When I started meditating, I thought it was a waste of time. "Why do I need to do that?" I thought. "What am I going to do sitting still and doing nothing for 20 minutes?" While I resisted meditating, I was also aware that I was not able to make changes in my life that I wanted to make. I wanted to be an entrepreneur but was too scared. I wanted to leave my job but was too scared. I was humbled by my own limitations and became willing to change and be open to the experience of meditating.

I began to shift my attitude to "OK, I'll try it. What could it hurt?" I had to force myself at first – making myself commit to spending 20 minutes a day in quiet time, sitting in meditation and doing nothing. I felt so resistant and fought my "What a waste of time" thoughts. I really didn't like it at first. I didn't like sitting still, especially when I felt the energy to get up and go. Day after day I disciplined myself to meditate. Over time, the resistance left me. I could sit still without feeling the urgency to get up and go. I became aware during one of these meditation times that I live my life in high-gear all the time. I am always doing something. I rarely took time to simply enjoy living my life.

As a result of my awareness of being on the go all the time, I began to make changes in my life. I began to enjoy meditation and being still. I found that I could sit still throughout the day without having the need to rush. In stillness I got a lot of clarity and this clarity helped me make the changes I wanted to make. This experience helped me move beyond my prior limits. I cannot completely explain why or how it works. But I can say that it works for me.

You may choose to get a meditation book that gives you a topic to contemplate or simply practice deep breathing exercises during meditation. My experience with meditation is to read a daily meditation and then focus on my breathing to clear my mind. I usually spend 10-20 minutes in stillness. There is no right or wrong way to meditate. The goal is to experience stillness within yourself.

Find a place, inside or outside, that is comfortable for you. You may like to set up the area with mementos that reflect what is important in your life. They can be pictures of yourself involved in your favorite hobby, of your children or family members, or items that remind you of your favorite places. My meditation area includes a candle, pictures of myself, affirmations I wrote, and some mementos that make my meditation space comfortable and uniquely mine. When I look at these mementos I feel pleasant feelings.

Do you meditate? If not, how do you feel about starting a meditation routine? Do you feel resistant? Excited about starting something new? If you already meditate, how does your meditation routine help you?

_____

_____

_____

What time of the day is best for you to schedule time to meditate? You may have to try different times to see what works best for you. First thing in the morning is best for me – before I have breakfast, before I shower, pretty much before I leave my bedroom. If I get up and go without taking the time to sit quietly and meditate, I never seem to get to it during the day.

_____

_____

_____

What are some mementos that you could include in your meditation area that make you feel good about you? Is there a picture of a sunset that you took when you were 15 years old that brings you pleasant feelings? Or a small piece of art that you painted when you were a child that your mother and father thought was beautiful? What about a picture of yourself enjoying your favorite hobby? Those are the kinds of mementos to consider – things that bring you pleasant feelings when you look at them.

_____

_____

_____

_____

Write down your meditation experiences for one week. This will help you find a time that works best for you when you can be least distracted. Consider the following questions: What were the circumstances when you chose to meditate? Were your surroundings quiet and serene? Did you choose a time when the phone rang and distracted you? Were your kids calling you? How did you adjust your time over the week to find a time that works for you? How did you feel during and after meditation?

Sunday: _____

_____

_____

Monday: _____

_____

_____

Tuesday: _____

_____

_____

Wednesday: _____

_____

_____

Thursday: _____

_____

_____

Friday: _____

_____

_____

Saturday: _____

_____

_____

| *Meditation helps me focus and feel serene.* |

Strengthen Your Spirituality

I didn't dream all this up on my own.
I found these ideas within myself – my spiritual self.

I cannot speak highly enough about the importance of spirituality in your journey. Spirituality is the association between your mind, body and higher self or higher power. Developing that association is what helps you change and grow.

Spirituality and religion are not to be confused. Religion is a formal set of beliefs, guidelines and rules that are set by others for people to follow. Spirituality is your own personal relationship with yourself – and your higher power or higher self. Spirituality is finding and following your heart. Spirituality is a feeling of wholeness of self, of oneness, perhaps the relationship between our heart and our soul – between what we can see in our lives and what we cannot see. I believe that spirituality is the foundation of the entrepreneur's journey.

We become spiritual through practicing a lifestyle that is important to us, one that gives us dignity and feeling of self-respect. This lifestyle includes practicing a balanced life – feeling emotionally balanced, taking time to meditate, be alone, be thankful and enjoy living life. Spirituality is the gift of the relationship with ourselves.

How does it feel to be spiritual? Each person's experience is unique. My experience of feeling spiritual is that it is a feeling of wholeness, of being a part of the universe – not just in it. I feel like I belong on my journey. Feeling spiritual also means feeling good, living fully, experiencing my life at the highest possible level each moment. Feeling spiritual is about feeling the relationship within myself and the world.

Do you feel spiritual? If so, describe what feeling spiritual means to you. If not, what do you think feeling spiritual means? Does it mean being and feeling peaceful? Does it mean enjoying your life?

_____

_____

_____

_____

_____

How do you envision feeling or being spiritual will help you in your business? Will it help you feel calmer? More grounded in being OK in the unknown? Better able to make change more readily and to trust the process of entrepreneurship?

_____

_____

_____

_____

_____

How do you develop and nurture your spirituality? Michelle found that working in her garden helped her feel a deeper connection with herself and with the world. She felt peaceful working in her garden and would choose to do gardening as a way to expand her spirituality.

_____

_____

_____

_____

_____

So many clients shared their experiences regarding the importance of prayer as an important part of strengthening their spirituality as they traveled on their entrepreneurial journey that I incorporated the topic into this exercise. To pray is to ask for spiritual guidance – to reach outside yourself to a higher being or higher belief. While prayer is a personal choice, many clients who felt emotionally challenged during their transition into entrepreneurship found comfort through prayer. Clients talked about prayer as part of a spiritual experience – not a religious ritual. It wasn't about saying specific prayers or going to church and having to pray. It was about being exactly in a moment and asking, sometimes pleading, for help. Some clients shared that they prayed and asked for help when they felt they ran out of options or because they felt stuck in their problem and couldn't find help in other ways.

Michelle had that experience. Prior to coming in for business counseling she was emotionally challenged by her business. She felt unfocused, confused and depressed about her business and its progress. She had an idea of starting a business but was struggling with how to start, what to do and where to go for help.

Michelle set up an appointment for business counseling and within the first five minutes of the appointment she burst into tears and said, "I've been praying for help with my business; you are the answer to my prayers." Michelle began business counseling with a willingness to change. Within the first few weeks, her confusion and depression lifted and she was able to set goals, focus and feel productive as she began designing her Web site, choosing a business name and deciding on products to sell. She participated in business counseling for several months and experienced personal and professional growth.

What role does prayer play? How does it work? Perhaps it works simply because it forces us to think about what we want and to crystallize those thoughts into concrete requests. Once we've asked our higher self or our higher power for help or guidance, it becomes easier to ask our colleagues or family or even ourselves for the items we need. From my experience in working with clients and from my own personal experience, I can share that prayer helped ease the hesitation and insecurity experienced in the transition into entrepreneurship. It helped clients move to a new level of awareness so they could find answers or answers could find them. While prayer helped some clients feel safe to proceed on a path that was unknown and full of uncertainty, prayer helped others soothe fears and have continued faith in their entrepreneurial journey. Prayer helped many clients find the direction they needed, the clients they needed and the advice they needed, simply for the asking. Prayer helped facilitate and guide the process of entrepreneurship.

You may choose to explore prayer as a tool to help you on your journey.

I am discovering my spiritual self.

Have Faith

I am ready in mind, body and spirit. I didn't just arrive here. I worked hard on my faith. I worked hard at believing in myself and I nurtured my desire to do this business. Deep in my heart, I know this business will succeed.

Faith plays an important role in entrepreneurship. It is especially helpful in dealing with the ups and downs of business. Faith is believing something that you cannot see. It could be belief in your business that is blossoming or belief in your abilities to grow as a human being. Faith is often supported or strengthened through spirituality, meaning that it can help strengthen your belief in what you cannot yet see when you believe that you are being guided spirituality – that situations will work out to serve your highest good.

Every client I worked with has had some degree of faith that they said helped them keep sane, helped keep them going and helped give them direction when they need it. Simply having faith that you are where you need to be and that everything you are experiencing is for your highest good will often serve to take the pressure off challenging situations.

What do you believe in that you cannot see? For example, I had faith that when I left my job, I was going to start a consulting project within two months. Judy had faith that she was going to get sponsors so she could start her radio talk show. Rose Lee had faith that she would find funding to continue producing her television show. Madeline had faith that her financial situation would improve. List three things.

1. _____

2. _____

3. _____

Faith has often been described as a muscle; the more you exercise it, the stronger it gets. How do you practice or strengthen your faith in what you cannot see? Do you meditate? Pray? Trust what you believe to be true? Minimize your negative thoughts?

_____

_____

_____

This exercise of strengthening faith is important because many times, as we walk through our entrepreneurial journey, we will need faith to step out into the unknown and believe in what we cannot yet see.

I continually strengthen my faith.

Respect Yourself

I do know some very important things – that taking good care of myself is important to my progress.

Respecting ourselves is important to preparing our minds, bodies and spirits for this journey. When we respect ourselves, we take good care of ourselves. For example, we think positive thoughts to respect our minds, we eat when we are hungry to respect our bodies, and we meditate, do random acts of kindness or spend time in nature to strengthen our spirits. You can strengthen your self-respect by acknowledging your mind, body and spirit as you travel on this journey.

The benefit of strengthening our self-respect is that we have the opportunity to experience more of our higher self, or spiritual self. The ability to experience our higher self can only be accomplished when our mind, body and spirit is respected, meaning that we take care of ourselves when we need to, not days or months or years later. It is when we take care of ourselves at all three levels – mind, body and spirit – that we experience this higher living. This level of self-respect will be valuable in other stages of entrepreneurship as well – such as before the money flows, when we need to have trust and develop our success path. It is this spiritual state that helps us experience a successful transition into entrepreneurship.

Not taking care of ourselves creates a negative domino effect. By not taking care of ourselves in one area, we hinder our progress in all areas. For example, I used to always have some health situation I needed to take care of – even if it was just maintenance – such as getting my teeth cleaned or getting a physical. I would always be a month or several months behind schedule to take care of my body. The domino effect began because not taking care of my body now affected me mentally. I would constantly remember that I needed to take care of myself but wasn't. These thoughts, because I continued not to take action, eventually turned into worry. And I would worry that because I hadn't been to the dentist or doctor in a long time, I may now have a physical problem, cavities, needed a root canal or crown. This mental strain, which was completely unnecessary and self-created, now affected me spiritually. My mental and physical self was not in balance, so my spiritual self was also not in balance.

Our goal here is to prepare our minds, bodies and spirits through self-respect. Personal and professional growth will be dependent upon how well we care for our minds, bodies and spirits.

We need to meet our body's needs for nourishment, fitness and care. This includes going to the doctor's office for screenings and when we are sick. It means taking care of our body's needs. As we have talked about, if we neglect ourselves in one area, we will neglect ourselves in others. It is by taking care of ourselves in one area that we can begin to take care of ourselves in all areas.

Do you have an exercise plan or schedule that you follow? If so, please describe below. If not, develop a plan. First, visit your doctor and get his/her stamp of approval on your exercise desires and routine. It is always a good idea to be aware of any physical limitations prior to starting an exercise program. Next, make a commitment to yourself to a particular exercise routine. The goal here is commitment – not rigidity. Do your best to make exercise a part of your weekly routine.

_____

_____

_____

_____

Look at your sleep patterns. Do you get enough sleep? Do your sleep patterns promote your well-being? Is healthy sleep a regular part of your life? Do you give yourself adequate rest time? Adequate time for sleeping and a consistency that your body can expect is important for a balanced life. My body functions best when I go to bed about 11 p.m. and wake up about 7 a.m. Adequate sleep optimizes my day. If you are not getting adequate rest, note what changes you will make.

_____

_____

_____

_____

Look at your eating habits. Is there anything that you would like to change? Do you eat a balanced diet? Eat occasional sweets?

Are you at your desired weight? Remember, our desire here is to allow as much free-flowing energy as possible and not inhibit our personal and professional growth. If you are not pleased with your eating habits, note below what changes you will make.

_____

_____

_____

_____

_____

Are you current with all of your medical care? For example, have you taken care of having your teeth cleaned on a regular basis? Are there any doctor's appointments that you need to make? If so, note what appointments you need to make and when you will make them.

_____

_____

_____

_____

_____

What about your physical self? Do you get your hair cut as needed? Take care of your appearance? Dress well and feel good in your clothes? If any of these areas need to be enhanced, note what changes you are committed to making.

_____

_____

_____

_____

Do you respect your mental self? Do you take breaks from mental work? Learn new skills? Not over-extend yourself intentionally by working beyond what you know is your limit? Do you worry and fret more than you wish to? Do you read stories that trigger worry, fear or depression unnecessarily? How will you take better care of yourself mentally?

_____

_____

_____

_____

_____

This exercise is helpful because when you get out of balance in one area of your life, you can evaluate what caused you discomfort and work to build your self-respect by not repeating a behavior that does not serve you.

I respect myself.

Your Life is a Balancing Act

Changes really have taken place in me and they continue. I am moving into a new spiritual dimension – a new dimension within myself. I have actually made enough changes in my life to allow time to read, to meditate and enjoy my life. Time has a sense of balance in my life. I don't feel like I'm trying to beat it or outwit it. Time just is.

Balancing our lives is important to preparing our mind, bodies and spirits for the life we desire. When we are out of balance, typically we are working too much. When this happens, we may lose our ability to distinguish the value in our work and we may feel stress. This stress sometimes pushes us to make hasty decisions or decisions that are not in our best interest.

The importance of balancing our life is to prepare ourselves for our lifestyle as an entrepreneur and not set ourselves up to repeat ineffective work patterns. We have to be careful that we are not becoming an entrepreneur simply to escape from our ineffective or out-of-balance work patterns. If we do not learn to balance our lives as we become an entrepreneur, we risk repeating this same pattern we had in our employee lives. Take Rob, for example. He had owned a business for more than fifteen years. He worked at least 12 hours a day, just about every day of the week. He was always busy. A few times a year, he played golf. He hadn't taken longer than a few days off work in more than ten years. Rob had set up his business to require more of him than was good for him. He had a heart attack in his mid-thirties and yet still did not balance his work time with his life. He did not see that his work habits negatively affected his life.

We can prepare ourselves for entrepreneurship by balancing our lives and getting used to experiencing this balance. Understanding why we are working more or less than we desire and why we are out of balance is important to our journey as an entrepreneur. Sometimes we can get clear about our work balance situation and determine if our work is in our best interest or not by slowing down, stepping back and making a decision about what changes we need to make.

Do you work because you just want money or because you enjoy working? Typically, if you are working for reasons other than the enjoyment of work, you will find yourself to be out of balance. This was my experience when I worked as an employee. I had to work at creating balance as an entrepreneur because my pattern as an employee was to work for the money rather than the enjoyment of the work. Describe why you work.

_____

_____

_____

_____

What actions can you take to balance your life? This can be a challenging exercise and often requires small changes over time. Can you take up a hobby after work? Not bring work home from the office?

_____

_____

_____

_____

_____

_____

Do you work more, less or as many hours as you desire? If you work more or less than you desire, why?

_____

_____

_____

_____

Is the circumstance forcing you to work more or less than you desire or are you choosing it to be that way? For example, do you continually choose to work in jobs that require all or most of your time?

_____

_____

_____

_____

What are your work habits? Do they help you move closer to your life vision or do they hinder you? For example, do you take time to enjoy pleasurable activities or are you always busy with work?

_____

_____

_____

Do you work in less of a capacity than you desire or are capable of? Are you choosing to do this? For example, Diana has two young children and is choosing to work a part-time, low-stress job while she is raising her family.

_____

_____

_____

Sometimes the motive in working in less of a capacity than we are capable of is fear of success, which is discussed in Challenge V. Take a look at why you work fewer hours or in less of a capacity than you desire. Look also to see if you are consistently out of balance. "See" what is underneath that and ask yourself what you need to do to change your behavior and balance your life, then make a commitment to change.

> **_I balance work time and free time._**

Express Gratitude

Thank you for uncertainty and clarity. Thank you for confusion and direction. Thank you for friends and family. Thank you for life and living.

As you prepare your mind, body and spirit by making changes in your daily life, it is important to express gratitude. Gratitude is being thankful for what you have today; your health, family, career, aspirations, serenity, positive changes or shifts in your life.

Being grateful for how we are changing or what we are receiving is a prerequisite to additional changes and growth. When we can recognize that what we are receiving is a gift and part of changes that we are consciously making, we can be thankful and experience gratitude. Gratitude, like confidence, can come either naturally or through a mind-altered state. We can make it a point to recognize one thing or several things that we are grateful for each day in order to open ourselves to additional personal and professional growth.

What are you grateful for today? What was important to you today? Did your health serve you? Did your child smile for the first time? Did you get a new customer? Did it rain enough to relieve a water shortage in your area? Was it sunny outside for the first time in a week? Did you incorporate your business? Did you make a decision about what kind of business you are going to start?

You may choose to do this exercise as part of your meditation routine over the next seven days. Freely express your gratitude. Use your journal if you need additional space.

Sunday: _____

_____

_____

_____

Monday: _____

_____

_____

_____

Tuesday: _____

_____

_____

_____

Wednesday: _____

_____

_____

_____

Thursday: _____

_____

_____

_____

Friday: _____

_____

_____

_____

Saturday: _____

_____

_____

_____

What did you experience from this exercise? Did you find that there were more things that you were grateful for than you thought? How did being grateful each day benefit you?

_____

_____

_____

_____

_____

I am thankful for everything in my life.

PREPARING YOUR MIND, BODY AND SPIRIT CHALLENGE REVIEW

Preparing our mind, body and spirit is important to our entrepreneurial journey. In preparing ourselves, we change ourselves and discipline ourselves to be our very best. We learn to balance our lives. We respect who we are and what we desire. We allow ourselves to change and grow.

Just like we prepare for a vacation or trip, we must prepare for our entrepreneurial journey. This preparation helps us know what areas we naturally have acquired and what areas we need to develop. With discipline we can develop the qualities that we need for our journey. The more prepared we are, the gentler and more fulfilling our journey will be.

Do you feel mentally, physically and spiritually prepared for your journey? What areas do you still need to develop? What areas of your life need to be maintained? It is important to distinguish between the two. For example, some areas we may improve with minor adjustments, while others will need continuous work.

What areas of your life need to be further developed? What are you still feeling resistant about preparing or changing? For example, you may feel resistant about being self-disciplined, meditating, or affirming your new beliefs.

1. _____

2. _____

3. _____

4. _____

5. _____

What areas of your life need to be maintained? Meaning that you have learned the lesson or changed the pattern and do not have any resistance to preparing yourself in these ways. For example, you may already be consistently getting adequate rest and eating right.

1. _____

2. _____

3._____

4. _____

5. _____

What area(s) do you need to focus on developing the most? What challenges you the most? These are the areas we need to make conscious efforts to change.

_____

_____

_____

It only takes one person to change your life...you.

Ruth Casey

CHALLENGE IV
OVERCOMING THE OBSTACLES

I can hardly believe how many obstacles I have had to overcome to get to today. I realize now that these obstacles were an important part of this journey. Each obstacle provided me an opportunity to get to know myself better and to affirm why I chose this path.

The journey into entrepreneurship is filled with obstacles – some we had before the journey, others we create along the journey. Regardless of when these obstacles appear, we need to recognize them and work through them. As we overcome each obstacle, we discover more of our uniqueness – more of who we really are. We persevere as we remove these obstacles or reduce their power over us.

This challenge points out the obstacles that many of the entrepreneurs I counseled experienced, including myself. Many clients did not realize that an issue they were dealing with was an obstacle until it continued to hold them back. Once an obstacle was pointed out and recognized, clients could decide how to deal with it.

This challenge teaches us that we can break through obstacles that either we couldn't break through before or didn't even identify as obstacles. With each obstacle we overcome, we find more of ourselves.

Obstacles are meant to be overcome. They teach us about ourselves. The more we know about ourselves, the smoother the transition into entrepreneurship.

We must overcome the obstacles...in doing so we find ourselves.

Anonymous

No More Excuses

I know I am a single mother. I know that I provide the only income to my family. But is that just an excuse, a reason not to pursue my dream? Not anymore. I owe it to myself to at least try – to give it my all. If things don't work out, I can always go back and get another job.

Excuses are so convenient. "I have too much going on right now." "I don't know what I really want to do." "I've done this job for 20 years." These are just a few of the excuses I've heard. Oddly enough, none of the people who used these excuses ventured away from them. They still use them to stay far from entrepreneurship.

What excuses have you been telling yourself? For example, I would tell myself that I needed to save more money before I could start a business or that my children were too young.

_____

_____

_____

Are your excuses true or false? Why?

_____

_____

What action will you take to eliminate your excuses? For example, if one of your excuses is that you haven't done anything because you don't know what you'd really want to do, then you can journal to learn more about your likes and dislikes, start reading books on business ideas, start attending small business seminars to get ideas. Write down the actions you will take to break through your excuses.

_____

_____

_____

_____

I no longer make excuses.

Getting Through the "Not Knowing" Phase

I can honestly say that for the first time in a long time, I do not know what to do about my career. I feel so much uncertainty. My gut tells me that things are changing, while on the surface it all looks the same.

The "not knowing" phase is the confusion phase of entrepreneurship. It is both normal and common. This phase has a purpose: to help you know yourself better.

Not only is this phase important, it is critical. It is part of the foundation of you and your business. After I completed a seminar on this topic, a woman asked, "What do I do if I don't know what to do?" I told her, "Start where you are. Learn more about yourself and be comfortable not knowing until you know."

It is helpful to read books, magazines and newspapers that relate to entrepreneurial business owners and experiences. How did other entrepreneurs find their way? How can you relate to them?

Allow yourself to "not know" and simply be OK with it. Describe what actions you will take to help you through the "not knowing" phase.

_____

_____

_____

_____

| *I am comfortable with uncertainty.* |

Set Boundaries – They Protect You!

> *I am in the process of learning some very interesting and important lessons. It doesn't matter how many hours I work, I'm still busy. The problem is me – not the job. I have a difficult time saying "no" and setting and maintaining boundaries.*

Our boundaries are like a moat around a castle. Just as the moat protects the castle, our boundaries protect us. Boundaries are our limits. They define what is and what is not acceptable to us. In a sense, they are like policies – guidelines for us to live and work by. Boundaries are especially important in entrepreneurship because they protect not only our business but ourselves. Therefore, without appropriate boundaries, we can create our own obstacles.

Often, we will be affected by not having a boundary before we recognize that we need one. Typically, we will recognize that we need a boundary through our feelings – anger about doing something we didn't want to do or frustration about saying yes to something that ended up being a bigger project than we expected. Feelings of manipulation are also common and important to recognize when we need to set a boundary.

There are two aspects of boundaries that are important: setting appropriate boundaries and sticking to them. Many entrepreneurs become challenged with setting boundaries in their businesses because they have been used to boundaries being set for them by their employers. Employers set boundaries by creating company policies and job descriptions. Entrepreneurs set boundaries by deciding what is good for them.

So how do you decide what is and what is not acceptable to you and your business? You may come across clients or people in general who will push you to your limit – to the place that we feel negative emotions. In this case, negative emotions are important because they tell us what is wrong. They let us know what is blocking us. Sometimes we have to be pushed to our limit and feel negative emotions to learn that we need a boundary. The realization that we need a boundary often comes when we say, "I've had enough." Whatever that circumstance is, it will repeat itself unless we set an appropriate boundary and stick to it.

As a new entrepreneur, Michelle became aware that she needed to set boundaries. Her family members continually asked her for favors and she always said "yes." She would agree to whatever they wanted her to do, even though she felt it was more than she was comfortable giving. It wasn't until she saw this similar circumstance show up with a client that she became aware of how she lacked the ability to set a boundary and say "no."

Michelle set a boundary with her family and began to say "no" to the things that she did not want to do. She also began to recognize what her limits were in her business. For example, she was working with a client who would call her in the evening and expect to talk about business and ask for assistance on short notice. These requests angered Michelle. She didn't want to talk with her client in the evenings and she preferred to receive notice of a request for assistance. So Michelle set these as boundaries and let her client know that she was available to talk weekdays from 9 a.m. until 5 p.m. unless there was an emergency. She also shared that she needed 24-hours notice for requests for assistance. Was it difficult for Michelle to set and stick with her boundaries? Sure it was. Her family and her client were angered, but only initially. Eventually Michelle earned respect for setting these boundaries and letting her family and her client know what was acceptable to her. By respecting herself, she gained respect from others.

What continually angers or frustrates you that you are allowing? Do you feel manipulated or disrespected? For example, do you continually say "yes" to projects that you don't want to do? Are you angry about agreeing to work extra hours? Write down the obstacles you experience that continually bother you.

1. _____

2. _____

3. _____

4. _____

5. _____

The exercise above will help you identify areas where you may need to set boundaries. Typically, these scenarios will repeat themselves, but the end result will be the same. We will feel an emotion that angers or frustrates us in some way. Anger is an important emotion that tells us what is going on with us even when we cannot yet identify what to change in our circumstance.

Setting a boundary may mean ending a professional relationship or changing the dynamics in the relationship. Boundaries are unique to you. There is no right or wrong boundary. They are simply guidelines that work to protect you.

List several boundaries that you would like to set. As noted above, Michelle set the boundary of not taking business calls after 5 p.m. and saying "no" to projects that she did not want to do.

1. _____

2. _____

3. _____

4. _____

5. _____

Expect to be challenged or tested when you set a boundary. When you tell a client who calls you late into the evening that you will not take calls after 5 p.m. unless it is an emergency, you need to mean it. Sometimes, a client will challenge you by repeating the old behavior such as continuing to call you after 5 p.m. You will need to respect your boundary by asking the client if his issue is an emergency and if not, tell him you will call him the following day. If you set a boundary and do not respect it yourself, others will not respect it either. Therefore, you can expect to be challenged as you overcome the effects of setting a boundary.

Pick one of the boundaries above and write down what you will say to whomever you are setting the boundary with. Being prepared helps you stick to your boundary.

_____

_____

_____

Remember to set your boundaries politely and not to over-explain. There is no need to give specific details as to why you are setting a particular boundary. Just share with whomever you are setting a boundary with that you need to do this for yourself.

> **I set and maintain healthy boundaries.**

Stop Comparing

I've got to stop comparing myself to others. Every time I compare myself to how much this one is making or how many new clients that one has – I feel less than. Like I am not doing it right or good enough. My way is enough – it's right for me. It's the comparing that is causing me the problem.

If you find yourself comparing your business, the money you earn, or your ideas to someone or something else, stop it. Even if you need to say, "stop it" out loud, stop comparing yourself to others. Comparing blocks you from accomplishing what you want to accomplish and seeing yourself for who you really are. Comparing blocks your uniqueness. Take Kent, for example. Kent compared his salary as an entrepreneur to what he thought he could make as an employee. He said to me in business counseling, "I could be making at least six figures if I worked for a corporation and here I am barely breaking even as an entrepreneur." This statement was contributing to blocking him from making progress on his entrepreneurial journey. It also contributed to lowering his self-esteem and taking on a negative attitude. Comparing leads us to dissatisfaction and usually makes us feel "less than" someone else. Comparing does not serve us in a positive or healthy way.

Kent was limiting himself by comparing himself and his circumstance to something that he really did not want to be doing anyway. Yes, he could be someone's employee, but I asked him, "Is that what you really want to do?" He said, "Of course not. I have been running my own business for five years." Again I pried, "So why are you spending energy comparing yourself to something that you don't want to be doing anyway?" He got the message and slowly began giving up his comparisons to a corporate salary. About eight months after this conversation, Kent's company was featured as the entrepreneur's showcase in a local business publication. He gave up comparing.

In what ways do you compare yourself or your circumstances to others? Do you compare salaries, jobs, clothes, cars, and ways of life?

_____

_____

_____

_____

How do you feel when you compare yourself or your circumstances? How does comparing serve you? For example, does comparing contribute to feeling superior or less than?

_____

_____

_____

_____

How will you eliminate or minimize your comparing behavior? For example, do you need to stop reviewing the newspaper's classified ads to see how much you could earn if you were an employee?

_____

_____

_____

When we stop comparing, we remove obstacles that block us from ourselves and discover more of who we are. What are you discovering about yourself that was blocked when you were comparing yourself or your circumstance to others? For example, I compared myself to others by thinking that I was less than because I didn't have an office and worked out of my home. When I stopped comparing, I discovered that I really liked working out of my home and that clients were glad to work with me regardless of whether I had an office or not. Write down what you are discovering about yourself as you stop comparing.

_____

_____

_____

_____

I embrace my uniqueness.

There's No Right Way

I want to work for myself. I want to create my world. Yet I keep thinking that other people have the "answers" as to how it's supposed to be done – that this is the right way and that is the wrong way. I've come to the conclusion that the right way is my way.

There is no right way. Neither is there the right time. Thinking that there is a right way is an obstacle. The right way is simply the way that works for you. I know people who, because of their circumstances, started a business while in debt. Others had it all planned out and still others quit their jobs, were fired or laid off prior to starting a business. Some do it all at one time, leaving the job then starting a business; others work while they start the business. In the ideal world we can take our time, save our money, have a plan and leave our job exactly when we are ready. However, we do not live in the ideal world. In the real world, there is no right way. The way to overcome this obstacle is to find the way that works for you.

Describe the "right way" for you to start or expand your business. Did you get laid off and now have the opportunity to start a business? Did you get fired, but have always wanted to run your own business? Are you in debt? For example, Gina was more than $30,000 in debt when she decided to start a company where she would install and service automatic teller machines (ATMs). She realized that if she accepted a job, it would take her more than 10 years to pay off this debt. She took a chance and started a business. It's been more than five years since she started her business and she has paid off all of her debt and is making a living doing what she enjoys. What is the right way for you?

_____

_____

_____

_____

_____

I am willing to find my own way.

Get "Most" Not "All" of Your Ducks in a Row

I just need to accept and know that my business is not going to be perfect.

Another common block for entrepreneurs is the desire for perfection. Perfection is an obstacle that can show up when we are unsure of ourselves. This is common when we transition into entrepreneurship. The challenge with perfection is that it masks feelings that are uncomfortable, not wanting to take risks and the need for control. Sometimes the desire for perfection is so strong that clients cannot rationalize taking risks, being OK with feeling uncomfortable or letting go of control, even if it is in their best interest.

The stronger the perfection block is, the longer it takes for an entrepreneur to make decisions, take risks, or start or enhance a business. Take Joshua, for example. He worked for a company as an employee for more than 25 years, was laid off and wanted to start his own consulting business, but couldn't get past the perfection block. He thought he had to do everything perfectly before he could start. For him, just getting set up was a perfection block. He couldn't decide on the business name, what address to use, what telephone number to use, whether to incorporate or not. The block was so strong that he missed opportunities that were before him. One time he met a potential client in an airport as part of a casual conversation but never followed up because he didn't have the business set up yet.

Joshua gained knowledge as his way of dealing with his need for perfection. He attended at least 30 seminars over six months. Then he started attending business-counseling sessions on a regular basis. He shared how he wanted to start his business but couldn't. One time he shared that all the knowledge he was gaining was working against him. He said, "I feel like all this information is chiseling away at my self-esteem." The focus of our counseling sessions switched to helping him deal with his perfection block rather than helping him gain business information. He was his own block, only now he knew it.

In order to let go of perfection, we have to do our part to prepare and feel our feelings, and then let go. It is kind of like taking on a new sport such as scuba diving. We get the gear, learn the basics, and then jump into the water.

Sometimes the difficulty in letting go of perfection is that we do not know that we will be OK. When we can't let go of perfection, we lack trust – either in ourselves or in the process. With entrepreneurship, some risk is required. Therefore, letting go of perfection is also required.

Is perfection in your way? If so, what is underneath the desire for perfection? Is it fear? Uncertainty? Loss of control? Know that it is easier to let go of perfection and break through this obstacle by knowing why you want it to be perfect.

_____

_____

_____

_____

How is perfection helping or hurting you? For example, trying to be perfect caused me great stress and anxiety. I was trying to control my life by being perfect.

_____

_____

_____

How will you allow yourself to make mistakes? How can you accept that mistakes are a part of learning? For example, can you be gentle with yourself when you do make a mistake by talking positively to yourself rather than saying hurtful things to yourself? Can you change the work "mistakes" in your vocabulary and think of them as opportunities? I choose to think of mistakes as learning opportunities. Learning opportunities do not have old meanings attached to them and they are easier for me to accept than mistakes. How will you allow yourself to make mistakes?

_____

_____

_____

_____

Since this is such a big obstacle for so many people, including myself, write a statement that gives yourself permission to make mistakes. Remember, if you are making mistakes, you are making progress.

_____

_____

_____

_____

I am willing to let go of perfection.

Breaking Through the "Not Enough" Obstacle

*The "not enough" feeling is so familiar to me – I have to work
hard at letting go of this old block.*

After working with several hundred entrepreneurs, I discovered
the "not enough" obstacle. This obstacle is similar to the desire
for perfection in that we may feel that we are unable to move
forward because of a feeling of a lack of knowledge, information,
material or even personal stamina. The difference, however, is
that the "not enough" obstacle makes entrepreneurs believe they
really *cannot* achieve what they desire because they are not good
enough or do not know enough. This obstacle is fear-based and
keeps us stuck until we break through it. The "not enough"
obstacle seems to affect entrepreneurs during times of transition –
the startup phase and the expansion phase. Fortunately, with
awareness, this obstacle is easily overcome.

How does the "not enough" obstacle work? It subtly holds
us back by making us believe that on some level we are not
ready. This readiness can be emotional, mental, spiritual or
physical. When a client thinks he does not know "enough,"
progress is halted. Often, business owners cannot see the "not
enough" obstacle within themselves because they believe their
limitations.

Undetected, however, the entrepreneur's "not enough"
obstacle can negatively impact business growth by continually
holding us back from opportunities that are presented to us. I will
share two examples below of business owners who had the "not
enough" obstacle and how they and their businesses were
affected.

Audrey came to see me about creating a brochure for her
new business. She was a graphic designer with a lot of design
experience and had several projects under way as a small
business owner. She knew she had the ability to work with
Fortune 100 companies; she just didn't have a brochure. A
colleague who knew the quality of her work had a connection

with the marketing director for a Fortune 100 company. She gave Audrey her name and phone number and told the marketing director that Audrey would call. Audrey never called. She had the "not enough" obstacle. She felt that because she didn't have a brochure, she couldn't compete.

Audrey missed an opportunity. She recognized that she had the "not enough" obstacle once she shared that even though she didn't have a brochure, she had experience, samples of her work, client references and other supportive documentation as well as herself – the greatest sales tool of all. Plus, she had a lead directly to the decision maker. This is an example of how strong the "not enough" obstacle can be.

Carlos came in for counseling because he wanted to expand his business. He shared that his business, a food production facility, operated at about 25 percent of capacity. When we began to discuss ways to grow the business and sales came up as an opportunity to expand his market share, he said, "I'm not a sales person." I shared with him that he might need to learn the skills necessary to do sales if he wanted to grow his business and increase the capacity of his facility.

You see, he had purchased the business four years prior and he had signed an agreement with product distributors. He didn't have to make any of the sales until now – when he wanted to expand his business. I talked with him about the "not enough" obstacle and how the lack of knowledge or information can hold us back from growing our business. He began gaining sales skills by participating in sales seminars and calling potential buyers and distributors. He also began working with a local college's marketing students who designed a strategic marketing plan for the expansion of his business.

When I spoke with Carlos about six months later, he was satisfied with the expansion of his business. He had several large contracts under way for distribution and recognized that he had moved beyond the "not enough" obstacle.

How you can relate to the examples above? Do you feel the "not enough" obstacle in any particular area of your life or business? If so, how is it holding you back? What do you need to do to overcome this obstacle?

_____

_____

_____

_____

_____

| *I know exactly what I need to know for today.* |

Know the Signs of "Overwhelm"

I don't enjoy feeling overwhelmed anymore. It is not a good feeling. I actually try to avoid situations that are overwhelming.

Being overwhelmed is a common obstacle in entrepreneurship and contributes to feeling stuck or blocked. Lisa stayed in feelings of overwhelm for years before realizing that she could recognize her signs of overwhelm and change her behavior. Her signs of overwhelm were feeling unproductive and unfocused. She shared that she would feel like she wasn't getting anything done all day. She didn't know how to get out of being overwhelmed. Each day, she repeated the same cycle. She learned to recognize that there were things she could do to learn about being overwhelmed and not return to this familiar but ineffective behavior.

My body responds differently to overwhelm. When I am overwhelmed, I feel physical symptoms such as a stomachache, headache, heart palpitations and sometimes difficulty sleeping. My body gets my attention whereas Lisa's thoughts get her attention. The point is that we both know that what we are feeling is overwhelmed – that we are entering a place that does not serve us well.

For others it might be sleeplessness or other forms of anxiety. Whatever the signs are, pay attention to them and modify your behavior so that you don't create an obstacle by being overwhelmed.

What are your signs of overwhelm? Do you lose sleep? Can't eat or forget meals? Give up your spiritual or quiet time? Stop exercising? Think obsessively?

1. _____

2. _____

3. _____

4. _____

5. _____

Once we learn our signs of overwhelm, we need to learn to stay out of overwhelm. Staying out of overwhelm means staying away from what does not work for us, staying away from our extremes. Extremes block our progress. Extremes are different for each person. They may include working extensive hours or not taking time to address our personal needs. Extremes usually result in some form of overwhelm.

Just as extremes are different for each person, being overwhelmed is different for each person. The problem with overwhelm and extremes is that they block our progress by affecting us either mentally, emotionally or spiritually. I have worked with many clients who were so used to being overwhelmed that they return to it on a regular basis – even though they know that it does not serve them.

Being overwhelmed blocks our progress and affects our energy level and our thinking. It affects the way we do business and how we feel about our business. What can you do to stay out of overwhelm? Do you take time for yourself? Time for fun? Time to balance your life? List at least five things.

1. _____

2. _____

3. _____

4. _____

5. _____

Being overwhelmed does not serve me.

Know that Struggle is an Option

One freedom that I've become aware of is that I don't have to struggle anymore. I realize that struggle is an option. I feel total freedom – there is nothing holding me back. I feel like I've crossed the bridge to freedom – crossed the bridge to life.

Sometimes struggling can become so much a part of our lives that we give in to it. We stay in our patterns of difficulty and live a struggle instead of living our lives. We forget how to live. Once we learn tools to let go of struggling and practice using these tools, struggle becomes an option – a choice. Until then, struggling remains an obstacle.

Eleanor came in for business counseling and shared how difficult her struggle was with her business and personal life. She started a business and was struggling financially. Her sister had recently died of cancer and she was the guardian for her handicapped nephew. Her situation was indeed challenging.

But Eleanor was perpetuating her struggle. When she came in for her second business counseling session, she apologized for being sweaty, saying her air conditioner had been broken for a long time and that she couldn't afford to fix it. She also shared that she turned down a consulting project because it was out of state and she needed to care for her nephew. Her nephew was in a home where people took care of him, but Eleanor didn't want to leave him. I suggested she reconsider taking this consulting project but she resisted.

A few weeks later, her financial situation had gotten worse. I shared with her what I believed to be true: that she was used to struggling. As difficult as it was, it was familiar to her. She had been struggling for years. What she didn't know was how struggling was an obstacle that could be overcome by making a choice. The consulting project she turned down was an opportunity to lift her from her struggles. It would have provided a secure income and helped get her new business going. We discussed how her nephew was being taken care of, and how she now needed to take care of herself.

She called the company that offered her the consulting project and the contract was still available. She took it. She worked during the week and flew home on weekends to visit her nephew. She began to realize that she didn't have to struggle any more.

Do you struggle about situations in your life? Why do you struggle with them? Are they situations in which you have done the best you can yet you continue to struggle? For example, Eleanor had done the best she could taking care of her nephew. She found good care for him, and yet she continued to struggle, even though she didn't need to.

_____

_____

_____

_____

_____

_____

What do you get out of the struggle? For example, Eleanor stayed in her struggle and people naturally felt sorry for her. When she let go of the struggle, she also let go of all the attention she got. Does your struggle absorb a lot of your time? Do you let a struggle run your life?

_____

_____

_____

_____

_____

What actions do you need to take to release your struggle? Do you need to give up worrying about a situation? Do you need to accept a job? Start a business? Let yourself be human and risk making a mistake? Try something new?

_____

_____

_____

_____

_____

_____

> *I can choose to be free from my struggles.*

You Are Worthy to Receive

I feel worthy and worthwhile. I feel like I know me and that is really what matters more than anything. I've grown a lot over the years – it is amazing how life continues to reveal itself to me.

Sometimes the blocks we face are in ourselves – our sense of self, our feeling of worthiness. We may have received verbal messages when growing up that were meant to discipline us that we took to mean we were not worthy or were not a good person. Pat was told throughout his childhood that he "was a bad boy." As an adult, Pat felt unworthy because he grew up believing he was "bad." Karen, on the other hand, received non-verbal messages that she was unworthy because of how her mother treated her. Karen's mother was always too busy to spend time with her.

The unworthiness that we feel can affect us personally and professionally. I worked with a gentleman who wanted a particular job for two years, and when he was promoted to that position, he turned it down. While he never came out and said he didn't feel he was worthy, it was obvious through his actions in wanting the job, improving his skills to get the job and then turning the job down when he got it, that feelings of unworthiness drove his decision.

From growing up Catholic and going to Catholic Church and school, I grew up saying out loud in church, "I am not worthy to receive..." I came to believe that yes, I am not worthy. I have spoken with many people who have had the same or similar challenge. While I am not challenging the religious faith about its ritual, I have decided that I am a worthy individual and that I am worthy to receive. We need to remove the blocks about our unworthiness and feel worthy.

It wasn't until I was in business for several years that the issue or worthiness rose to the surface. I found it difficult to charge what I was worth. I did not know how to set a price for my services that reflected my value. Once I became aware of this issue, I was open to changing my messages about worthiness and be taught how to charge for my worth. It was a necessary but difficult lesson.

Do you feel worthy to receive goodness in your life? If you do not know, take a look at your past and see if you had messages, either verbal or non-verbal, where you felt worthy or not-worthy. Consider the examples above. It may be helpful to work on this exercise as part of a meditation where you are still and open to clarity about your feelings of worthiness.

_____

_____

_____

_____

_____

Another way to look for the issue of worthiness in our lives is to see how others treat us. Basically, however we are treated is how we expect to be treated. So if we are treated well, we expect to be treated well. If we are treated poorly, then we don't expect to be treated well. I noticed this issue of worthiness to be especially true when I was a sales person and worked with a sales person named Phil. While all of my clients paid their bills, Phil's clients did not. He continually went to meet with clients to collect money and often was not paid. I wondered, "Why do my clients pay their bills and his clients don't?" I realized that Phil didn't expect to be treated well and so he wasn't. How do others treat you?

What will you do to feel worthy or enhance your feelings of worthiness? Often, this requires action. For example, can you begin treating yourself better, ask for help, stand up for yourself, or take a risk?

I am worthy to receive.

Break Through the "Big" Business Mindset

I am learning that if I take steps each day toward my goal, I can accomplish what I desire.

Very often, a "big" business mindset can be an obstacle when we start or expand our business. We think the business is supposed to start or expand a certain way and so we allow that to block our progress. A "big" business mindset can lead to procrastination. Often, we do not need every resource we think we need to get started. One client, Ted, started his business with a fax machine in his son's bedroom. That fax machine was his initial investment. The rest of his business was based on his prior experience in this particular field and his client contacts. Ten years later, Ted's business grossed more than $5 million annually and is located in a 17,000 square-foot building.

Do you have a "big" business mindset that is blocking your progress? What do think you really need to start or expand your business? Do you need money? A store? More experience?

1. _____

2. _____

3. _____

4. _____

5. _____

Of the five items listed above, could you start the business or expand the business with just one or two of them? Is what you describe as "needs" to start or expand your business really just blocks or steps to your progress? For example, if you said, "I need $50,000 to start my business," challenge that statement.

What if you started with \$15,000 or \$5,000? Create different scenarios for each of the needs you listed above. The goal of this exercise is to see if there are any other scenarios in which you can start or expand your business that you have not considered.

Scenario 1:

_____

_____

_____

Scenario 2:

_____

_____

_____

Scenario 3:

_____

_____

_____

Scenario 4:

_____

_____

_____

Scenario 5:

_____

_____

_____

| *I make progress one day at a time.* |

Build Your Support System

I have built a strong network of people in my life – business friends, tennis friends, dancing friends, diving friends and friends to call and talk to. I feel good about the network I've built.

We may try to go it alone but sooner or later we will realize that we need support and lots of it. Without a strong support system, we create unnecessary obstacles for ourselves. A strong support system is important to deal with the challenges of entrepreneurship as well as to share the excitements of the journey. Just as athletes who train for the Olympics have the support of coaches, family and friends, so it is with those of us who are on an entrepreneurial journey. Why is our support system so important? Without it, we can stay stuck in our obstacles. Without it, we tend to try to solve for ourselves the problems that need the effort of friends or colleagues. Support systems help us move forward. Many times, the clients who came in for business counseling shared that they never talked about their challenges with anyone before. They had been carrying this burden themselves. Trying to solve problems alone makes our journey difficult.

Many clients said, "I can't believe I am telling you this" or "I never told anyone this before." By talking with someone, they began to break through whatever it was that challenged them. One of the reasons clients made so much progress during business counseling was that they learned to be part of a support system. They learned the importance and value of sharing their challenges.

Reach out and build or expand a support system. You may find support in a family member, a colleague or another person on the entrepreneur's journey. Plan to meet with them to share what is going on with you and your business.

Diana is part of my support system. I call her when I have a problem I cannot solve by myself. When I tell her my problem, she makes suggestions and helps me find a solution. Another person in my support system is Angela. We work with each other to grow our businesses, primarily by developing marketing strategies. We typically meet every two months and stay in contact via e-mail.

Who is in your support system and what kind of help can they give you? How do they support you with business issues? How do they deal with your fears and emotional issues? Do they help you formulate business strategies? Do they stimulate your creativity or help you solve problems? Write down the names of your supportive friends, family or colleagues and the type of support they provide.

Support Person	**Support Provided**
1. _____	_____
2. _____	_____
3. _____	_____
4. _____	_____
5. _____	_____

We will likely need to seek resources beyond friends and family. We need a lot of support and different kinds of support when making changes in our lives – especially when these changes relate to our stability, our financial future, and our livelihood.

The more I am willing to recognize my need for support, the more options I see with regard to support. Many people that came to me for business counseling said they never knew the services were available, even though the services had been offered for more than fifteen years in the same location. When we become open to support, we will find support.

Just as a grown tree that has been transplanted needs supportive braces to hold it in place while its roots grow deep into the soil, a business owner or prospective business owner needs support as he or she ventures into entrepreneurship. We are venturing into new territory. There are many governmental and nonprofit organizations that support entrepreneurs and small business owners with seminars and counseling. Investigate what business support systems are available. Try several out until you find an organization that meets your needs.

What kinds of business support do you need? Do you need advice on starting a business? Guidance on importing products? Help with getting a loan?

1. _____

2. _____

3. _____

4. _____

5. _____

Review your list and find out what nonprofit or governmental agencies can support you. Typically, the county you live in funds business assistance programs. Do some research. Ask your librarian. Seek out the resources that can help you. Write down the agencies you found through your search.

_____

Agency Name

_____

Contact Name and Title

_____

Phone Number

_____

Service(s) provided

_____

Agency Name

_____

Contact Name and Title

_____

Phone Number

_____

Service(s) provided

_____

Agency Name

_____

Contact Name and Title

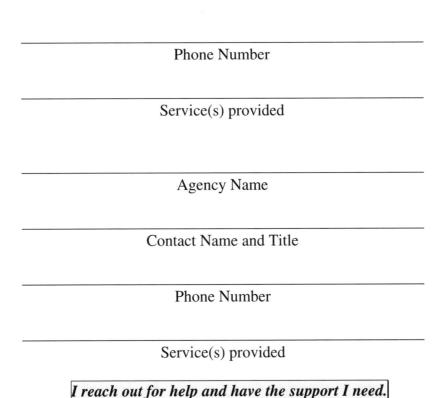

Phone Number

Service(s) provided

Agency Name

Contact Name and Title

Phone Number

Service(s) provided

I reach out for help and have the support I need.

Start Asking for Help

*Sometimes, I feel like I am weak when I ask for help. I am
learning it is a sign of strength, and much more.*

If you need help, ask for it. You've built a support system now
start using it. Many times clients would come into business
counseling feeling alone and isolated. Even though they had
people to talk to, it wasn't until they got to the point of despair
that they even thought about asking for help. The reason that
asking for help is often not an option until we are desperate is
because on some level, we don't want to look "weak." We might
think people will think less of us if we ask – as if we are
supposed to know the answer to our problems. We are human and

it is unrealistic to assume we always have the answers. The bottom line is that if we ask for help we will usually find it.

Expect to need help. Remember, we are traveling on a journey in all-new territory. We have never been to this place before. Ask for help if you need it.

Emily was challenged financially with her business. She had not generated any revenue for six weeks before she finally reached out for help. She came in for business counseling. We went over several ideas to help generate business. We also set goals. Two weeks later, she returned with her goals and a fresh attitude toward her business. She shared how resistant she felt to ask for help when it was the one thing she needed most to do. She accepted that she was getting through a challenging time and that it wouldn't last forever. She realized that by asking for help, other opportunities opened up. In addition to getting business counseling, one of her colleagues offered to design a Web site for her at no cost.

When you need help, do you ask for it? What does it take for you to get to the point that you ask for help? For example, do you suffer a lot before you ask for help? Do you try one time or 100 times to solve the problem before you ask for help?

_____

_____

_____

_____

If you do not like asking for help, explain why. What are the feelings beneath this obstacle? Do you feel weak or that you think you should be able to solve whatever problem it is without help? If you do ask for help, are you satisfied with the time it takes you to ask for help or could you learn to ask for help sooner?

_____

_____

_____

_____

_____

_____

Describe three situations in which you will ask for help. Do you need help developing a business plan? Or setting up QuickBooks? Do you need someone to talk to about a family problem? The reason this "ask for help" exercise is so important is that once we realize that we need help, we break through the obstacle and find new options.

1. _____

_____

2. _____

_____

3. _____

_____

I ask for help when I need it.

Be Aware of Non-Supportive People

Every time I leave Mike's house after he is supposedly helping me with my business, I am in tears. Is that support? I don't think so. I am writing a letter to him to discontinue our business relationship.

We create unnecessary obstacles for ourselves by talking about our business with non-supportive people. Our conversations with non-supportive people can actually hold us back and inhibit us from moving forward on our entrepreneurial journey. I have seen this many times in business counseling. Often, people starting on their entrepreneurial journey have great ideas, but when they share them with non-supportive family or friends, their ideas get shot down before they even have a chance. Chuck was in the medical field and wanted to open a retail store. He came in for counseling and felt frustrated and confused because when he told people about his idea, they said, "Oh, why do you want to do that? You could make a lot more money practicing medicine." I suggested he only tell his ideas to people in his support system. Telling non-supportive people about a business idea is like handing a baby to someone who does not know how to hold it. A baby is defenseless, new and can easily be injured if held the wrong way. And so it is with a business idea. It needs to be shared with people who will support it.

When there is lack of support between two people in a relationship, learning to support each other is of particular importance. Phil was in this situation. He had been in business several years. His partner got mad at him for working long hours and he got mad at his partner for not managing her spending habits. They communicated regularly, sometimes disagreeing about how they supported each other. They discussed their anger toward each other as well as what they wanted to accomplish with the business as a couple. They learned how to support each other and what each other needed for support. Phil needed his partner to manage her spending so they set spending guidelines.

She asked Phil to work fewer hours and so she agreed to help with some of the administrative tasks.

Another example is a woman who shared how her excitement turned to depression after telling a non-supportive person about a situation. Michelle shared with a non-supportive person her excitement about getting her first order. This person replied, "What's one order? Is that enough to keep your business going?" Michelle no longer tells this person her company business. She cannot risk being involved in negativity.

Be selective with whom you share ideas. Remember, you are sharing an extension of yourself, so you are exposed. Keep non-supportive people at a distance from your business and/or ideas.

Some people may not be able to support us even though we continually go to them for support. Decide which people cannot or will not support you mentally, emotionally or spiritually. The goal of this exercise is to help you overcome the obstacle of returning to someone for support who cannot or will not support you. Be careful not to blame them for not supporting you. They don't need to overcome this obstacle – you do. Who is not able to support you in your business venture? Why?

1. _____   _____

2. _____   _____

3. _____   _____

4. _____   _____

5. _____   _____

If you are in a relationship with someone who is not supportive, are you willing to talk with your partner about the importance of their support? How can you support each other? After talking with your partner, list five ways you will work to support each other.

1. _____

2. _____

3. _____

4. _____

5. _____

I immerse myself in supportive relationships.

Dealing with Resistance

I've felt this resistance for over a week now. I keep doing what I need to be doing anyway. Eventually this feeling will go away.

Resistance, ah yes. Do you feel it? It's that feeling that comes up for me just before I am to do something different from what I am used to doing. I have consciously worked through this feeling hundreds, if not thousands, of times. The first time I became aware of feelings of resistance was when I was starting a 400-hour internship for my bachelor's degree in social work. The professor said, "There is resistance to active learning. Be aware of it as you go through this internship."

What is interesting about resistance is that it doesn't come up until I've already felt excitement about whatever I want to do differently. The way I recognize that I'm feeling resistance is to recall when I felt good about what I feel resistance toward. This is how I know it is resistance, not just something I don't want to do. Recently I facilitated a planning session for a client and when I signed the contract and prepared for this session, I was excited.

But as the time came to do the planning session, I felt a lot of resistance.

My job is to feel the resistance and do what I need to do anyway. I have felt resistance in many scenarios – before giving seminars, before preparing a final report for a client, before facilitating a meeting, before making an uncomfortable call. Once I master whatever skill I am learning, resistance leaves me. The lesson has been learned. Expect to feel resistance as you learn new behaviors and transition into entrepreneurship. It's part of the process.

What do you feel resistant about? For example, are you resistant to setting up a business? Leasing new office space? Calling potential clients?

_____

_____

_____

What is your pattern of dealing with resistance and will this pattern work for you in entrepreneurship? For example, if you delegated the work you felt resistant about to an assistant in the past, how will you get those things done now that you do not have employees?

_____

_____

_____

Describe how you will deal with resistance if you've identified that your patterns will not support you in entrepreneurship? For example, will you set a deadline for yourself to achieve what you are resisting? Will you block out time in your day to deal with issues that you resist?

_____

_____

_____

| *I accomplish things even when I feel resistance.* |

Stop Feeding Your Ego

Being an entrepreneur is so difficult sometimes. My ego misses feeling important by having a title, office, and nice salary.

While our egos may have been satisfied as an employee – because of status, prestige or even a nice salary – they may be threatened as an entrepreneur. Our egos do not like any threats to their status. And becoming an entrepreneur can definitely be a threat to the ego.

Our egos can block our progress if we don't watch out. Remember, we are learning to overcome obstacles and getting to know ourselves better. This means that we need to learn how to deal with our egos.

My friend Diana, who was an independent consultant for more than six years, accepted a job in another part of the state for a large company. She thought, or her ego thought, that she needed to accept a high-paying job in order to get more valuable consulting jobs. She accepted the job, and she, her husband and children moved to the other side of the state. It turned out that she had a difficult time adjusting emotionally to working in a salaried position again. She said that she felt trapped because she had signed a one-year contract and if she quit, she would then need to reimburse the company more than $10,000 in moving expenses.

She shared with me that she felt she "sold her soul" in order to make a bigger paycheck. She finished her year and went back to being an independent consultant. She shared with me later that she has outgrown being an employee. Her ego didn't need that experience any longer.

Many of us who chose to give up paychecks, offices and status had to deal with our egos. We gave up these things that were important to us then to experience deeper more fulfilling lives. Somehow we knew we could experience more of who we were by making this transition. The position we had, with all its perks, didn't satisfy us on that deep level. As one client shared with me, "My job contributed to a disconnection from myself." Once we become aware of this, even if we have known for a long time but tried to deny it, we can then make the choice that we are going to pursue this deeper experience of ourselves.

While we will go back to the ego at times – for some it is wanting that satisfaction to fit in again, to compete, to have the nice office or perks – we will have those moments and can expect them. Know you can always go back. You may need to in order to learn what you need to learn to go forward.

How does your ego serve as an obstacle? Does it think that status is important? Material things are important? That you are not important without a title, office or income?

_____

_____

_____

_____

_____

Think about what your ego wants. Does it help you or hinder your progress? For example, my ego would prefer I made a consistent income, so I have to be careful not to fall into this trap of believing that I am not important unless I am making a consistent income. If I buy into that statement then I feel depressed and less productive in my work.

_____

_____

_____

How do you deflate the influence of your ego when it hinders your progress? For example, sometimes I write about how I feel in my journal and other times I talk with supportive friends about challenges that come up regarding my ego.

_____

_____

_____

My ego can feel good about me becoming an entrepreneur.

Beware of "Stigmas"

I am so hard on myself. I need to lighten up and stop labeling myself with false truths about myself. I am capable of becoming a successful entrepreneur.

A stigma, according to Webster's dictionary, is a mark or obvious trait that is characteristic of a defect. Sylvia called to ask for business direction with regard to starting a business. A few minutes into the conversation, she shared that what she really needed help with was overcoming the stigmas – what she had come to recognize or label as a defect within herself. She went on to share that she had no problem selling other people's products or service but when it came to selling her own, she was having trouble.

We are so quick to judge ourselves and give ourselves a label of defect, aren't we? Here Sylvia had the courage to venture out on her own and start a business and had already labeled herself as having a defect. She had just started a business so selling her own product was completely new to her. If we spent years working for others, yes, it will take time for us to learn how to work for ourselves. I don't believe it is a defect at all. Most behaviors are learned. When we start labeling ourselves, we take on a new challenge – overcoming the "stigma" we place on ourselves in addition to learning the behavior to counteract whatever is challenging us.

Sylvia did not make an appointment to come in for business counseling. It was my belief that she felt embarrassed about labeling herself with this stigma of being "defective."

Are you creating any additional burdens by labeling yourself with a stigma? If so, what is the label? Sometimes the "not enough" obstacle shows up here – not smart enough to start or grow a business – or the feeling of being stupid for having made a mistake.

_____

_____

_____

_____

If you have labeled yourself with a stigma, what will you do to release it? For example, if you think you don't know how to sell, what will you do to change this thought pattern? Will you write down affirmations about your prior success in selling? Will you talk with supportive people about the stigmas you have?

_____

_____

_____

_____

I am capable and willing to be myself.

OVERCOMING THE OBSTACLES CHALLENGE REVIEW

Overcoming the obstacles is an ongoing process and is unique for each person. Some people may be more challenged by one particular obstacle than another. I like to think of obstacles as opportunities for growth – ways to get to know ourselves better. Obstacles don't always feel good to work through. The fact that they don't "feel good" is usually an indicator that a particular obstacle is being overcome – that a particular lesson is being learned.

The most important lesson in overcoming obstacles is to recognize, confront and work through them. Feel the resistance but work through it anyway. Remember, once we learn the lessons, we do not have to repeat them. It is the same with obstacles – once we learn how to deal with them, they will not be obstacles any longer. To continue to grow personally and professionally, we will, however, continue to experience new obstacles. The lesson here is that you have learned how to overcome them and can overcome new obstacles that challenge you.

What obstacle is the most challenging for you to overcome? Making excuses? Setting and sticking to boundaries? Perfection? Struggling? Worthiness? Comparing yourself to others? Look back over the challenges in this chapter to refresh your memory and write down the obstacles that are most challenging for you. Remember, we learned in an earlier chapter that by admitting and accepting our situation, even our obstacles and challenges, we can begin to overcome them.

_____

_____

_____

_____

Are there other obstacles that you recognize within yourself that
were not outlined but that you need to address? If so, list them
here.

_____

_____

_____

_____

_____

_____

What did you learn about yourself that you didn't know before
you started this challenge?

_____

_____

_____

It is important to know how you deal with obstacles so that you
can overcome ones that challenge you in the future. What is your
process to work through situations that challenge you? For

example, I work through obstacles by first feeling and listening to my feelings. Then, I like to call a support person or write about the pros and cons of a particular situation, how it will affect me, why it is bothering me, what my options are, etc. I then make a decision about how I will handle a particular obstacle and take action. The benefit of this process is that you can learn the lesson the obstacle is teaching and grow from the experience.

_____

_____

_____

_____

> **Do not follow where the path may lead.
> Go instead where there is no path and leave a trail.**
>
> **Muriel Strode**

CHALLENGE V
BREAKING THROUGH THE FEARS

I feel like I am finally moving through these fears. I am arriving at "the other side." The fear of money, fear of the unknown and all these other fears are finally going away. I am facing them and working through them one at a time.

Fear is one of the main challenges to break through while becoming an entrepreneur. The night before I was to facilitate my first corporate planning session, I was filled with fear. While I had worked with this client on several consulting projects, this project was new. My excitement about being contracted and being given the opportunity to facilitate this planning session had turned into fear. I began to question myself and the questions came faster than I could keep up with: Can I really do this? Do I even know what I am doing?

I was challenged by "what if" scenarios such as, "What if I can't do this?" "What if something goes wrong?" I wanted to turn around, turn back. It seemed as if every fear I ever had returned one night to challenge me. As the night went on, I came to the conclusion that I was going to do my best and that I was there to share my expertise.

When I awoke in the morning, I felt calm. The serenity actually surprised me. I felt as if a storm passed through me. I couldn't believe all the fears were gone. I said a prayer in the morning, asked for guidance and went to the planning session. None of my fears materialized and the results of the session were even better than either my client or I anticipated.

> ## Our greatest glory is not in never falling, but in rising every time we fall.
>
> **Confucius**

What Are You Afraid Of?

I can't believe how much fear I had to work through to get here. Lots of fear! Fear of running out of money, fear of failure, what ifs, out-of-control fears and thoughts. I feel like I've worked through these fears – cleaned out those "closets" per se – and prepared myself for the next step.

I was more frightened than ever before as I transitioned into entrepreneurship. I was stuck in fear. I couldn't deny it and I didn't know how to deal with it. My fears seemed so real, so big and so unsurpassable. They kept me in my present circumstance – in a job that I didn't want to be in. I remember feeling and saying that this transition into entrepreneurship was more difficult than anything I ever experienced in my life, including getting a divorce, which I had experienced a few years prior. I was shocked, really, that my fear was so great and equally shocked that with all the books out there about starting a business, none of them addressed what I was going through emotionally.

I experienced my greatest fear at the most difficult time – when I made the decision to quit my job but had to still work there while saving the money I'd need to begin my entrepreneurial journey. Though I had not yet told anyone I was planning to leave, I knew I was leaving.

I needed a new approach to deal with my fear. One day while sitting in my meditation area and feeling scary feelings, I decided to make a list of my fears. I took a hard look at my fears, particularly as they pertained to transitioning into entrepreneurship. I started by simply writing at the top of the page, "What am I afraid of?" I listed my fears. One-by-one they were revealed; they were on paper now so I couldn't deny them anymore.

What I discovered from putting my fears in writing was that fear of not having/making enough money, which I thought was my No. 1 fear, was actually not what I was most afraid of.

My No. 1 fear was actually the fear of the unknown – not knowing what was going to happen when I left my job. The security and comfort of bringing home a regular paycheck was so familiar and comfortable that the thought of not having a paycheck was nearly inconceivable.

Once I knew that the fear of the unknown was my biggest challenge, I began to talk about it with people who supported me in my journey into entrepreneurship. Laura, a woman I admired and who was successful making this transition into entrepreneurship, listened to my fears and offered her experience and support. I began to change my attitude toward the unknown by accepting it as part of the journey. I began to see the unknown as a positive aspect of my life rather than something to be feared.

The second fear on my list was one that embarrassed me – it was the fear of being or going crazy. How could I talk to someone about that? I wanted to deny this fear, but denying it wasn't going to work, I knew that. So I was willing, once again, to talk about and challenge this fear with my supportive friends. This fear was very challenging to confront. Sometimes I thought the idea of starting my own business might just be a crazy idea. I questioned myself, "Was I crazy for even thinking about leaving a good job and starting a business? Was I crazy for thinking about going into business for myself while raising two children on my own?" I was just going to have to find out.

The problem with this fear was that I wasn't sure if it was true or not. I felt depressed much of the time staying in a job I didn't want. Here I was wondering why I was depressed and why my emotions were erratic when I was not being true to myself. I realized that I spent more than 40 hours a week doing something I didn't want to do, but pretending that I did and telling myself that I must like this job because I was good at it. By confronting this fear, I came to the conclusion that the only reason I was still working at that job was to get a paycheck, and that was not a good enough reason anymore.

Those were my two biggest fears – the fear of the unknown and the fear of going or being crazy. Surprisingly, money was third. I challenged this fear by saving money before leaving my job. I set a goal to save the equivalent of six months living expenses and set a date upon which I would leave my job. I circled the date in my calendar and drew stars and balloons to signify my freedom.

Being afraid wasn't going to be enough to hold me back anymore. The experience of dealing with my fears was greatly lessened by listing and then challenging each one. This process helped me break through my fears and continue moving toward entrepreneurship.

The exercise below helped me break down each fear and essentially dissolve it. I got to see each fear for what it was. Fear was no longer something to be afraid of but rather an opportunity to become a stronger person, to get to know myself better and to accomplish what I knew I could accomplish.

What scares you about where you are on your entrepreneurial journey? Make a list. Do not judge your fears, just write them down.

1. _____

2. _____

3. _____

4. _____

5. _____

6. _____

7. _____

8. _____

9. _____

10. _____

Now, look over the list and prioritize your fears. Continue with the following exercise for the fear(s) that scare you the most.

1. What scares you the most? Why does it scare you? I needed to write about the fear of going crazy. I wasn't sure I would be OK once I made the transition into entrepreneurship. Why was I afraid of going crazy? What did going crazy mean to me? Could I make this transition into entrepreneurship while feeling that I might go crazy? I actually wrote about it a lot. You may find the need, once you begin to acknowledge and write about your fears, that you need to write about them more than just through this exercise. Use your journal to write even more. Write down what fear scares you the most and describe why it scares you.

_____

_____

_____

_____

_____

_____

2. How can you lessen this fear? The fear of running out of money was a big one for me. It had me believing that I would end up homeless or living on the streets. I needed to write in my journal and talk with my supportive friends to

get to the root of this fear. I got to the root of this fear by asking myself, "How could I lessen this fear?" I decided that having six months of living expenses saved before leaving my job would lessen my fear, and it worked.

_____

_____

_____

_____

_____

_____

3. Describe the worst-case scenario with this fear. What is the worst thing that can happen regarding this fear? The worst-case scenario was that I would need to give up my entrepreneurial venture and get another job. While this is a simplified and rational worst-case scenario, it did not come to me until I went through this entire process.

_____

_____

_____

_____

_____

_____

4. What can you do so that the worst-case scenario does not happen? With my money fear, I decided I could get a part-time job if I got down to two months of savings while still working toward my entrepreneurial venture.

_____

_____

_____

_____

The goal of this process is to create rational solutions for irrational fears. When we break our fears down in this way, our fears are lessened and become manageable. This is the way that I was able to break through my fears and move forward.

I am becoming stronger by working through my fears.

Feel Your Fear

I feel frightened. I feel like such a baby. I hate being afraid. I've learned though, that when I allow myself to feel afraid, instead of pretending I am not, the fear goes away.

While it is motivating, fear can also be paralyzing. Getting in touch with fear, as well as other feelings, will give you the opportunity to feel and release fear.

Most clients come to me surprised to learn that feeling their fear is important. How and why should it play any role? The truth is that what we feel and believe both play a vital role in our entrepreneurial journey – our feelings help define who we are and what our needs are. We get to know ourselves by feeling our fearful feelings and acknowledging them.

The fears that we feel create opportunities for us to become stronger. Each time you feel afraid, think about the strength you are gaining by feeling afraid. We can move through our fearful feelings by feeling them.

Expect to feel fear. I find that entrepreneurs don't like to talk about their scared feelings – it is as if they are ashamed of having these feelings. These feelings are normal – let me repeat – they are normal! Let yourself feel afraid. Write in your journal about feeling afraid. Tell someone in your support system that you are afraid. It is OK and important to feel your fear. Remember, you gain strength by allowing yourself to feel afraid.

The next time you feel fearful, return to this exercise and write about it. What is the fear about? What triggered the fear? What does the fear feel like?

_____

_____

_____

_____

_____

_____

Each time you feel afraid, go through this exercise and then complete the steps in the prior exercise (What are you afraid of?) to break down your fears.

I feel and release my fearful feelings.

Let Go of Worry

I am giving up worrying – has it ever worked for me? No. I am going to work at going with the flow and not worrying – just to see what happens.

Many of our fears turn to worry when we do not deal with or face them. Worry is an ineffective way of dealing with problems. Unfortunately, many people still worry when dealing with problems. Worry is one of the most common challenges that I help entrepreneurs deal with through business counseling. Like other negative emotions, excessive worry can lead to health problems, sleeplessness and a multitude of other problems that hinder entrepreneurial progress.

Many years before I became an entrepreneur or even before I knew that I wanted to be an entrepreneur, I visited a mental health counselor named Ed. At the time, I was suffering from panic attacks, low self-esteem, a poor sense of self and many other life challenges. I did not realize until he pointed it out that I worried a lot, and about many things. During one session, Ed said, "Worry is a luxury that I cannot afford." That simple saying stayed with me. I could not afford to worry, either. While it took me a long time to understand and develop tools to let go of worry, I am now free from this negative habit.

As negative and as destructive to our bodies as worry is, it is accepted by society. Some people believe we are supposed to worry. Take parents, for example. Are we a better parent because we worry? I remember feeling guilty because I was able to go to sleep while my son, then 17, was still out with friends. I would hear other parents say that they cannot go to sleep until their child is home. Does that make me a bad parent because I didn't worry? One time after returning from visiting relatives, my son said, "Aunt Karen worries about everything. She's nervous all the time." My son was not only able to recognize that someone worried a lot but also how it affected her.

According to Webster's dictionary, to worry is to torment oneself with or suffer from disturbing thoughts. Sometimes worry is like a gray cloud that looms overhead and blurs our focus, makes us nervous. How can we effectively start or run a business with all of this negative emotion? Our goal in letting go of worry is to recognize that it does not serve us.

One of the ways that I let go of worry in both my personal and professional life was to develop a better relationship with myself. I didn't know myself very well. I actually didn't want to know myself very well because I was afraid I would find out I was inadequate or that something was wrong with me. I got to know myself through journaling, learning about my likes and dislikes, and taking actions in my life that were good for me, whether I wanted to take them or not.

By getting to know myself, I learned to trust myself and to trust that if I had a scary thought, that's all it was, a scary thought. My scary thoughts included thoughts that I might go crazy, that I would end up financially broke and that I could not cope with the changes that an entrepreneurial venture would bring. It didn't mean that I would or had to act on those thoughts. I didn't know how to believe in myself. I was able to function without believing in myself by not taking risks or venturing into new experiences. I stayed guarded so that I wouldn't enter life situations that would challenge my lack of a belief in myself. One of the reasons I didn't go scuba diving for 17 years was because of fear and worry, fear that I might have a panic attack or not be able to handle myself, fear that I would be out of control in some way. It wasn't until I got to know myself better and began to make the decision to believe in myself that I was able to go scuba diving again.

Another tool that I used to let go of worry was to trust the process – to trust where I was in my life and that it was right where I needed to be, whether it felt good or not. How could I trust the process? This was a big dilemma for me. I discovered through counseling clients that it was a big dilemma for many entrepreneurs, so much so that the theme of this book's last chapter is about trust. I realized that I was trying to control the process, not trust the process. By trying to control it, I was consumed by worry that things would not work out right. I discovered that I could not trust the process so long as I tried to control it. When I realized that controlling the process didn't work, I decided to try trusting the process, letting life unfold on its own terms rather than on my terms. Life works much better this way.

Worry plays a big role not only in our mental wellness but in our businesses as well. Letting go of worry helps us transition into entrepreneurship. Think about it. If you were setting out for a journey, how would you prepare? How would you learn to deal with potential obstacles? Would you need to learn new skills? Get into better shape? Learn about where you plan to travel? That is what the entrepreneur's journey is all about – preparing ourselves, improving ourselves and letting go of things like worry that are not useful or effective.

I would not be at this point of my life if I had not let go of worry, gotten to know myself, accept myself, love myself and learned to believe in myself and trust the process.

What do you worry about? Losing your job? Starting a business? Having enough money to send the kids to college? Not paying your bills? If your worries flow out of you, you are ready to be released from them. Use your journal if you need extra space and start writing and releasing your worries.

1. _____

2. _____

3. _____

4. _____

5. _____

6. _____

7. _____

8. _____

9. _____

10. _____

Look back over the worries above. What do they have in common? For example, do you worry about situations in the future or situations in the past that you fear will repeat themselves? Are they situations that you have no control over? Situations that have never happened? Write down what your worries have in common.

1. _____

2. _____

3. _____

4. _____

5. _____

What are some actions you can take to begin letting go of worry and fear? For example, can you take a risk? Challenge an old fear? Do something that you wouldn't do before? Consciously decide not to worry any more? Part of my ability to break the pattern of panic attacks was doing things that scared me, like going diving. By doing these things, I strengthened myself emotionally and lessened my fears and worries. What are some things you can do to lessen your worries?

1. _____

2. _____

3. _____

4. _____

5. _____

While I didn't bring the subject of spiritual guidance into my business counseling sessions when talking about letting go of fear and worry, my clients almost always did. I was providing business-counseling services in a non-religious university. It is because so many clients shared the importance of believing in spiritual guidance in dealing with fear and worry that I decided to write this section. Many clients shared that they could not have ventured on their entrepreneurial journey alone, that the fears and worries were too great. Their belief in a God or spiritual guide aided the process for some and provided the path for others. If letting go of fear and worry is difficult for you, consider re-reading the spiritual exercises in Challenge III.

> **I have no need to worry. All is well.**

Fear of Success

Can I be afraid of success? I think so. Why else would I be feeling afraid of a really positive outcome? This fear of success is an interesting feeling - similar to my fear of failure, which I am very much aware of. I am just going to have to feel it and keep going.

While many don't speak about it, the fear of success is real. I have talked with many clients who have had this fear. I had it as well. The fear of success stems from a feeling of vulnerability, exposure and/or lack of self-confidence. The fear of success usually comes up when we have an opportunity to move to a new level of our professional lives, such as becoming an entrepreneur. How do we deal with this fear? By feeling it, acknowledging it and not letting it stop our progress. In other words, feeling afraid but doing what needs to be done anyway.

I became aware of how powerful the fear of success was while working with Michelle. Michelle had recently returned from a trip oversees and decided while she was there that she wanted to import herbs into the United States. Shortly thereafter, she completed some market research and began to explore her startup options. At about that time, I received a call from a colleague who is a reporter who was looking for people starting an import/export business. I told him about Michelle.

When I told Michelle about the opportunity to get some publicity for her idea, she was excited and scared at the same time. I gave her the phone number of the reporter. She called me the following day to say that she couldn't call. She was afraid and she wasn't sure why. We talked about her fear and she described it as being afraid of being known and exposed. As if there were greater expectations of her. Having dealt with the fear of success with other clients, I mentioned that what she may be feeling is the fear of success. We discussed the fear of success and she agreed that while she hadn't thought of it that way, that is what it was. The fear of success was real for her and it stopped her progress. While having a story written about her could be great for business, it did not feel good to her. She realized that when she was an employee, this issue never came up. Working for someone else somehow shielded her. Now, as an entrepreneur, she was exposed.

Michelle acknowledged her fear of success, became aware of just how strong it was and how, as a result, she did not take an opportunity that could give her business exposure. The fear of success wanted to hold her back, and not risk exposure. She eventually made the call, but it was too late for that story, that time. But the experience helped her confront her fear of success.

Experiencing the fear of success is very common – expect it, feel it, talk with someone about it and walk through it. My fear of success comes up every time I move into a new experience in my business. Is it challenging, yes, but I know it will pass. It is only a feeling.

Can you recall feeling the fear of success? Know that the fear of success may reveal itself in different ways. It may show up as feeling fearful, resistant or exposed. It may also show up through procrastination. The fear of success can be different for each person. Describe any feelings or any experiences you have that may relate to the fear of success.

_____

_____

_____

_____

How do you work through the fear of success? Do you accept the feeling or try to ignore it? Michelle worked through her fear of success by first admitting that she had the fear, talking about it and then taking action.

_____

_____

_____

_____

Pretend you are experiencing the success you desire. What feelings come up for you? Feeling scared? Excited? Confident? Write about how success feels to you.

_____

_____

_____

_____

What scares you the most about being extremely successful? For example, is it becoming well known? Is it actually achieving what you desire? Is it that people will have greater expectations of you?

_____

_____

_____

I am experiencing success as part of a fulfilling life.

Fear of Failure

I realized today that I often fear the worst. I feel like if I fail, my life will be ruined. Is that really true? It's time for me to start questioning this fear and seeing if it is real or not.

Like fear of success, fear of failure can keep us from making progress. Fear of failure however, seems to be recognized and accepted by society while fear of success isn't. While many identify with the fear of failure, it can be a self-fulfilling prophecy if not addressed and resolved.

Pam's fear of failure contributed to her business failure. Pam owned a retail store. Her business was in financial trouble. She contracted my consulting services to increase her profitability by identifying potential markets and revenue streams, and develop a marketing plan. Pam's problem was not so much that her business wasn't doing well but that she was frozen by her fear of failure. Her fear was so strong that she was not able to make decisions that would save her business. I made several cost-saving suggestions, such as temporarily reducing her staff and cross-training her employees. Her fear of failure was so strong that any change to her current situation became a potential threat to her. She talked and cried about how strong this fear of failure was for her and how it was limiting her ability to be successful. Pam let her fear control her decisions and unfortunately, closed her business shortly thereafter. She and her three employees were all out of work partly because of Pam's fear of failure.

Fear of failure, like all fears, is a feeling, and that is all it is. If we let it, fear can control us and stop us from making decisions, resulting in what we actually feared to begin with – failure itself.

We can move through the fear of failure without letting it paralyze us. By expanding our understanding of the word *failure* we can dissipate our fear of it. Whenever I feel what I call "fear sickness" creeping into my life, I make an effort to stop the fears by first feeling and acknowledging them and then challenging them. I acknowledge the fear by admitting that, yes, I am feeling the fear of failure. Once I acknowledge it, I can decide what I want to do. Typically, I challenge or confront the fear by writing in my journal about it. I ask myself, "What triggered this fear? Am I working too much? Am I out of balance? Am I overtired?"

Just as a snowball gets bigger when you roll it down a mountain, fears get bigger if you allow it to escape and create problems in your life.

What does fear of failure feel like? How does this fear show up in your life? Does it stop you from making decisions such as starting or expanding your business? Does it feel safer for you to stay in your job, even though you want to make a change?

_____

_____

_____

_____

How do you deal with your fear of failure? Do you accept it and work at confronting it or do you try to ignore it? If your tendency is to ignore the fear, how can you begin to accept that you are fearful and challenge the fear? For example, can you talk with a supportive friend about this fear? Can you ask yourself why you feel the fear of failure?

_____

_____

_____

Sometimes our thinking regarding failure scares us. We may equate failure with death or not being able to function in this world, and so we do everything we can, including staying at jobs we do not like, to avoid this potential tragedy. What does failure mean to you? Do you believe that you will fail if your business fails? That you will not be able to survive?

_____

_____

_____

_____

_____

Look at how you described failure. How can you expand your understanding or thinking about failure so that it will work for you instead of against you? I used to equate failure with the inability to function in this world. That understanding was not going to serve me as I ventured into entrepreneurship. I learned that many successful entrepreneurs experienced various levels of failure before they finally succeeded, so I decided to equate failure with opportunity. I now see failure as creating an opportunity for me to explore.

_____

_____

_____

_____

It has been said that if we can find the root to our fears, we can be freed from them. What is at the root of your fear of failure? I discovered that the root of my fear of failure was that if I failed in business then I, as a person, would be a failure. Once I realized this was how I saw failure, I was able to revise this understanding and learn that I was not a failure if my business failed. As a result, I gave myself permission to fail. Can you give yourself permission to fail?

_____

_____

_____

_____

| *My fear of failure no longer serves me.* |

Answer Your "What If"s

I feel scared and fearful. The "what ifs" are scaring me. I guess this is something I just go through when I am scared. I am afraid of giving a speech. I told myself today that I don't need that much fear anymore. But that didn't work. I needed to answer my "what if"s.

"What if"s are scenarios or situations that we create in our minds. While they are there to protect us from potential danger, they can hold us back if we let them. Typically "what if"s cause anxiety or fear until we confront them. One of my old "what if"s was, "What if I don't make enough money?" Once I noticed that this "what if" was not leaving me even though I ignored it, I challenged it and finally answered it. Well, I thought to myself, I first needed to decide what "enough money" meant. I decided it meant being able to live on what I made without going into my savings. Then, I decided to take this "what if" further and see how many months I could live if I did not make enough money. I had a six-month reserve of savings, plus I had a credit line and credit cards. I dissolved this "what if" about not making enough money – at least temporarily. So now I had a response to this "what if" when it came up in the future. Other "what if"s were right behind this one such as, "What if my business doesn't succeed?" "What if I don't get any clients?" I tackled them the same way I did the first – by answering the question.

We can learn to use "what if" scenarios to help us evaluate our options and then choose how to respond. I like to think of "what if"s as stop signs. When we stop at a stop sign, we check to see if the traffic is clear before proceeding. We don't just sit at the stop sign and worry that cars will come; nor do we stay clear of roads with stop signs. We proceed with caution until we develop our ability to use stop signs. "What if"s give us the opportunity to make sure it is safe before we proceed.

Bruce, who we talked about in an earlier chapter, was breaking through his fear of moving to Spain when the "what if"s set in. Bruce said during a counseling session, "What if I lose my passport?" We answered it: Make two copies, leave one with family and keep one in a suitcase. If the passport is lost, take the copy to the American Embassy and get a new one. He said, "What if I can't find a job in Spain?" We answered it: Set up a budget and a time frame to get a job. If he did not get a job, he could come back to Florida, work and save money, then go back to Spain later.

This exercise taught Bruce how to answer his fears with a logical response rather than a fearful response. Had he not learned how to answer his fears, they might have grown into larger fears or become worries and he would not have gone to Spain. He did go, and as far as I know, he is still there.

What "what if"s do you have? They may not come to you immediately. Sometimes they show up only when you begin to expand into a new level and fear comes along for the ride. These fears, regardless of whether they are business related or not, need to be confronted. Typically, if we have "what if"s in one area of our lives, we have them in another. Once we practice confronting these scenarios and we see that they need not hold us back, our mind will not create as many. Write down as many "what if"s as you can think of regarding any fearful thoughts that you have. Use your journal if you need to.

1. _____

2. _____

3. _____

4. _____

5. _____

Take each of the "what if"s listed above and challenge each. What if the situation you describe does happen? How could you help yourself? What actions can you take? For example, with Bruce being worried about losing his passport, he could make copies of it to minimize the impact of losing it. Create three scenarios that will help you deal with the "what if" in the event that it does happen.

What if No. 1:

_____

_____

Actions:

1. _____

2. _____

3. _____

What if No. 2:

_____

_____

Actions:

1. _____

2. _____

3. _____

What if No. 3:

_____

_____

Actions:

1. _____

2. _____

3. _____

What if No. 4:

_____

_____

Actions:

1. _____

2. _____

3. _____

What if No. 5:

_____

_____

Actions:

1. _____

2. _____

3. _____

The goal in this exercise is to help you confront your "what if"s and know how to deal with them when they come up. Anytime you have a "what if" come to mind, write it down, along with three possible ways you can deal with it, and then decide on a course of action.

> **_I can handle my "what if"s._**

Watch Out for Fear Cyclones

I saw myself "spinning" today – fears going round and round. I hate that. I have to learn to catch myself before I let my fears start spinning me around. It drains me just to keep thinking about my fears over and over.

Cyclones spin wind, gain energy and dominate the atmosphere. Fear cyclones spin fears, gain energy and dominate our minds. A fear cyclone gains strength and has the power to cause a lot of destruction. Fear cyclones typically start from an unsolved problem or situation and are usually fear-related. They can start in different ways. They may start by being afraid and not taking any action or they may start by letting our fears get out of control by thinking about them obsessively.

In order not to enter a fear cyclone, we need to be aware of what situations or fears we typically obsess about. Are we fearful about the future? Do we fear for our safety? Fear cyclones are habit forming. We can try to resolve our fears this way, though this process is not effective.

What is important to learn is that we have a choice about entering a fear cyclone. As soon as we sense our fears beginning to spin – that our fearful thinking is dominating and potentially clouding our minds – we need to stop. Make a conscious effort to either change behavior by doing something different or physically telling ourselves to stop thinking about those fears.

I used to have fear cyclones on Saturday mornings. That was the morning that I slept in and had unstructured time. At that time in my life, I had not yet learned effective ways to deal with my fears, so unsolved fears and problems showed up when my mind was clear. If I stayed in bed on Saturday mornings and entered the fear cyclone, I ended up with a headache by the time I got out of bed. One time, I realized that these fear cyclones were not solving any of my problems or resolving any of my fears. They just made my fears and problems seem bigger and drained me emotionally. I began getting out of bed when I woke up on Saturday mornings. I had to be cautious not to enter thought cyclones during the day by saying "stop" out loud – when I was alone. My thought cyclones had their greatest impact when I was alone – so that was the time I needed to be wary of.

If we stop a fear cyclone early on, before it gains strength, its detrimental effects may not affect us. These detrimental effects include depression, loss of sleep, lack of energy and fearful living. Rose Lee experienced the effects of a fear cyclone after she completed her taxes and realized that she didn't make as much money in the year as she thought she had. Even though she had savings to supplement her income, she plunged into her fears of not being able to make it in her entrepreneurial venture. The thoughts that started this fear cyclone were, "How am I going to make a living on this amount of money?" "What if my income doesn't increase next year?" "I don't think I can run my own business anymore." She allowed her thoughts and fears to negatively spin her into a cyclone that took her several weeks to recover from.

Rose Lee came out of the fear cyclone when she accepted her circumstance. There was nothing she could do to change the amount of money that she made the prior year. She also accepted that she was fortunate in having savings and that she wasn't going to go broke overnight unless a catastrophe happened. She saw that fear cyclones are often irrational fears. They are not true, although they appear to be and feel real. She made the decision to continue in her entrepreneurial venture despite the low revenue. This helped her feel empowered by her circumstance rather than feel she was a victim of it. She also came out of the fear cyclone by putting together an action plan to move forward. She asked herself how was she going to make more money in the coming year, what she would do differently and what goals she would set to work toward.

Fear cyclones can be habitual, meaning that when the same fearful thought comes into our minds, we repeat the same behavior unless we do something differently. The exercise below can help break the pattern of entering fear cyclones by becoming aware of the fearful thoughts that lead to them, identifying the circumstances that trigger these thoughts and then taking specific actions to modify our thoughts.

Can you recall specific fears that turn into fear cyclones if you let them? For example, fears about not making enough money, not getting any clients or trying to figure out a specific problem? Once you identify the fear that leads to fear cyclones, write down the circumstance that triggers these thoughts. Sometimes the fear cyclone can happen the other way around. Repeated actions or circumstances stimulate fears that turn into cyclones. For example, I used to let my checking account balance go below a certain dollar amount. When it did, I entered a fear cyclone about not having enough money. This was a predictable pattern for me and still is if I am not careful about my thoughts and actions. Fear cyclones can be completely irrational. In my example, I would enter that fear cyclone even when I had money in a savings account, in a 401(k) program and invested in mutual funds. The question then becomes "What do I need to do to release these fears so that I do not enter these fear cyclones?" There were several things I did. For one, I worked at not letting my checking account go below a certain dollar amount. If it did, I transferred money from my savings account into my checking account. I also linked my savings to my checking so I can transfer funds online or through an ATM machine. Complete the following exercise to help you break through your fear cyclones.

Fear that leads to fear cyclones:

1. _____

What triggers this fear?

_____

_____

Actions to take to prevent future fear cyclones regarding this particular circumstance:

a. _____

b. _____

c. _____

Fear that leads to fear cyclones:

2. _____

What triggers this fear?

_____

_____

Actions to take to prevent future fear cyclones regarding this particular circumstance:

a. _____

b. _____

c. _____

Fear that leads to fear cyclones:

3. _____

What triggers this fear?

_____

_____

Actions to take to prevent future fear cyclones regarding this particular circumstance:

a. _____

b. _____

c. _____

The purpose of this exercise is to strengthen our ability to deal with our fears. We are working to capture creative energy, not let it leak into fearful thinking and fear cyclones. Just think of being free from fear cyclones, free to use that energy instead for something creative. How much value would that add to your life? How much time and creativity could be used for something positive?

> **I think healthy thoughts.**

Practice Meeting People – Lots of Them

I went to a networking function tonight. I didn't really want to go but I knew it would be good for me. It wasn't that bad. I met new people and had fun.

Another area that people often experience tremendous fear is meeting new people and networking. Meeting new people in business can be intimidating, especially when you are early in your entrepreneur's journey. One reason is because we feel vulnerable and do not want others to see us this way. Feeling vulnerable can stimulate our fears about meeting people.

We each have different ways of dealing with the fear of meeting people. Even though Patrick had a tremendous fear of meeting people, this problem did not present a problem for him until he went into business for himself. As an employee, he accepted jobs where he didn't have to deal with too many people. Now in his own business, his fear of meeting people challenged him like no other fear had before. I realized how scared he really was after making several suggestions that he go and meet new people at networking events. He wouldn't even go when a colleague invited him and offered to go with him. He was stuck in fear. What did he need to do to break out of his fear of meeting people?

We each need to answer that question for ourselves. For some, it just takes practice meeting new people and gaining networking skills. For others, like Patrick, the fear of meeting people was more deeply rooted in an unresolved problem from another area of his life. In Patrick's case, the problem was alcoholism. While he thought he got rid of this problem by not drinking any more, the fears of meeting people would not leave him. Patrick decided to deal with this unresolved problem from the past by starting to attend Alcoholics Anonymous meetings. Once he began resolving the problem in this area of his life, his fears about meeting people went away.

Be open to opportunities to meet new people. If you are afraid of meeting people, write about it. Use the space below and continue in your journal. Get to the root of this fear. Why are you afraid? What is it about meeting people that scares you? Do you think they will find out something about yourself that you are trying to hide? I felt like this at one point in my life so I know it is a real and valid fear.

_____

_____

_____

Start exploring and attending networking functions. You can begin to identify which networking functions would be beneficial by finding out what organizations support you personally and professionally. You may still feel uncomfortable meeting people in new situations. Expect that. But you can still function, and indeed move forward when you feel uncomfortable.

Even though networking can take place on your doorstep, in the food store, in a networking meeting or on an airplane, you can make a conscious effort to network by attending networking functions. Here are a few places to consider:

➢ <u>Chambers of Commerce.</u> These organizations are havens for networking opportunities. Their whole role is to promote business growth and they do this by offering events where people can meet and do business with each other.

➢ <u>Trade Associations.</u> There is an association that supports just about every industry. Whether you are going into construction or consulting, there is a trade association you can explore.

➢ <u>Nonprofit Organizations.</u> Contact your favorite nonprofit organization and find out about upcoming fundraisers.

I am open to meeting new people.

BREAKING THROUGH THE FEARS CHALLENGE REVIEW

The purpose of the Breaking Through The Fears challenge is to see how powerful our fears are, how they can hold us back if we let them and how we can build our strength by learning to see them as opportunities and break through them. It is also important to note that if we practice these new ways of dealing with fear, we become less fearful and naturally gravitate to a positive approach to deal with challenging situations rather than to a fearful approach. We learn to recognize that how we deal with our fears is a choice – and the choice is ours.

I realize that had I not changed my thinking in how I dealt with my fears, I would have never become an entrepreneur. It would not have happened just because I decided I wanted to be an entrepreneur. I tried to do it without challenging my fears but it just didn't work. I learned that if I wanted to pursue an entrepreneurial venture, I had no other choice but to deal with my fears and become stronger as a person.

Knowing how fearful I was when I started this journey, and where I am today in dealing with fear, I know that it is possible to deal with and break through our fears. If I can do it, you can do it.

What did you learn about yourself from having examined your fears? For example, did you learn that you are more or less afraid of one fear than another?

_____

_____

_____

_____

Typically, once we start to challenge fear, it begins to dissolve. Which fears dissolve or are being dissolved from having completed these exercises? Do you feel like any of your fears have lessened? If so, what will you do to continue lessening your fears?

_____

_____

_____

_____

_____

What tools do you find most effective in dealing with your fears? Writing about them? Talking about them? Challenging them by taking action?

1. _____

2. _____

3. _____

4. _____

5. _____

**Do the thing you fear
and the death of fear is certain.**

Ralph Waldo Emerson

CHALLENGE VI
LEAVING THE COMFORT ZONE

I am getting ready to file the paperwork to start my business. Part of me screams, "What are you doing? What about security, your job, health insurance, the kids? Why do you want to leave the comfort zone?" That's the scared part of me. The other part of me is cheering me on – congratulating me – loving me into wholeness. This part of me believes in what it cannot see. It has faith in me.

One day, it will happen. We leave our jobs for good. The difference this time is that we don't leave for a higher salary, a better title, more perks or greater clout. We leave to discover more of our potential, what we are truly capable of.

This transition of leaving the comfort and security of a job is challenging for many people. It requires faith in the unknown, and becoming comfortable with uncertainty. Many of us had years of training to be an employee. We were taught how to follow rules, who to report to, where we worked and even when. I had a difficult time letting go of the security of a job, even though I had known for a while that I was primarily there for the paycheck. I was addicted to security in a sense. My identity was wrapped around a job.

While I knew three years before I finally left my job that I wanted to be an entrepreneur, I did not make the break until I felt slighted by my employer. Even then, it took two attempts at leaving and returning before I could leave for good. I discovered that the more successful I became and the more money I made, the more difficult it was to leave.

Regardless of how and why we transition out of an employee role and into an entrepreneurial role, we are leaving what we are comfortable with and are venturing into the unknown. We may feel a new array of feelings that we haven't felt before. And if we do not have faith that we can get through these feelings, we will likely return to what we know, a job, even temporarily. Mike, a successful accountant who became an entrepreneur, had that experience. After admitting that he was low on money and needed to return to a job, he shared the following comment, "I have never had my confidence shaken like it has been from going out on my own." He went back to a job – but only for a few months. It is amazing just how vulnerable, how exposed we can feel when we leave the comforts of a job.

> ## When you experience uncertainty, you are on the right path – so don't give up.
>
> **Deepak Chopra**

Trading Security for "Uncertainty"

It was worth trading my security and unhappiness for uncertainty and aliveness.

We are stripped of the "corporate cover" as the veil of security in our jobs is lifted and we come face-to face with ourselves – our faith and belief in who we are. We see ourselves and feel our vulnerability and for many of us, it is a completely new experience. This ability to face ourselves is the greatest challenge and the greatest opportunity we have in entrepreneurship. How do we do this? We learn to have faith in uncertainty and in the unknown. We find security within ourselves instead of outside ourselves. The idea of security we get from a job can be an illusion. If we think we are secure in our job, then we don't confront uncertainty.

For me, feeling uncertainty and being OK with it took me a long time to understand. I'd ask myself, "Why is uncertainty so difficult for me?" I got the answer – even though it was an answer I didn't like. I didn't have faith in myself. I lacked a belief in myself, had little self-esteem and didn't feel secure within myself. Wow! What a blow to my ego. But it was true. And once my truth was revealed to me, I could begin to do something about it. The irony of this revelation was that I saw myself as self-assured and good at what I did. What I realized was that I borrowed "security" from my employers; it was on loan to me. The security that I felt when I worked at a job was never mine. It was not at the root or core of my being, where it needed to be. I hadn't yet developed these qualities within myself.

The awareness that I was borrowing my sense of self from my employer was monumental in terms of understanding why I had such a hard time leaving my job. I recognized and accepted that I lacked a sense of security in who I was. This acceptance brought an understanding as to why I went back to school for all those degrees – and sought higher-paying jobs and promotions. The better I got at my job, the more security I needed, so it was a vicious cycle that I didn't even realize I was in until I tried to get out.

As you choose to experience uncertainty, you are transformed merely through the experience of choosing the unknown path. The unknown path is actually the journey to one's core or soul. Clients develop faith in themselves and discover who they truly are through this experience. They begin to have a new level of living and freedom.

Each person's set of securities is unique. For some, it is salary, hours, perks, 401(k) programs and insurance. For others, it is the less tangible things such as familiarity and predictability. Whatever it is, it is important to recognize what makes us feel secure, so that we can at least be aware of our feelings when we let go of this security. We can make it through this phase. Even though I have felt uncomfortable through many "growth spurts," the most uncomfortable time was leaving the security of my job and making my initial transition into entrepreneurship.

Describe what makes you feel secure about being an employee. For example, I felt secure with a salary I could depend on each week, quick results from my hard work, job satisfaction, knowing that I had a place to go every week, and being recognized for a job well done.

_____

_____

_____

_____

_____

What is motivating you to let go of these securities and make the transition into entrepreneurship? What motivated me was the passion I felt to be my own boss. I didn't act on this passion until I was uncomfortable in my work situation. Write your motivation for leaving your job and transitioning into entrepreneurship.

_____

_____

_____

_____

_____

What does the uncertainty of leaving or having left your job feel like to you? Is the feeling of uncertainty negatively or positively affecting you? For example, are you losing sleep or sleeping better? Do you feel freedom or fear?

_____

_____

_____

_____

_____

_____

If you have a difficult time dealing with uncertainty, as so many entrepreneurs do, ask yourself why. Look deep for the root or the cause of this discomfort. I suggest that you ask yourself this question and not expect an answer right away. A good time to ask the question is during your meditation time, before you go to bed or right when you wake up. The answer will come to you when you are ready to hear it. Or you may consider writing about it in your journal or talking with supportive friends. Write below your discovery of why uncertainty is difficult for you.

_____

_____

_____

_____

_____

Once you acknowledge that uncertainty causes you discomfort or challenges you, you can begin to do something about it. For example, if you discovered that you need to work on your self-confidence, you can go back and work on the self-confidence exercises in Challenge I, or look to other sources and ways to develop your self-confidence. The same holds true for any discovery about yourself that you have. The goal of this exercise is to recognize where your discomfort regarding uncertainty comes from, what the root of it is and then take appropriate action. It is important to mention that changes we make in our lives take time. It may not be enough to work on self-esteem or self-confidence through one exercise. Some exercises may need to become part of your daily routines. Write down what actions you will take to work on the roots of your discomfort regarding uncertainty.

1. _____

2. _____

3. _____

4. _____

5. _____

I am comfortable with uncertainty.

Getting and Staying Out of Our Own "Trap"

I feel like I am trapped in this job. Am I trapped or did I create this trap?

Some of us may have looked upon our jobs as a trap, something that we needed to escape from. I felt that I was in a job trap. The reality was, however, that no one made me accept or continue to work at my job. I accepted my job willingly and it was my responsibility to get out of it. No one could do for me what I needed to do for myself.

How do we get out? It may be the only job we've ever known or the only type of work we've ever done. We may not know what we want to do and so we stay in our job. We may be scared and so we stay. At what point do we leave? That answer is different for each of us. We each come to our own understanding of when it is time. We each develop the faith in ourselves that we need. Often, this time comes when we discover that we've created our own trap and that we are only stuck to the degree that we believe we are stuck. What we come to discover is that we are our own trap – not the job. The job only helped us stay in our trap.

That was my feeling and the feeling of many of the clients I worked with. Once we understood that we created our own trap, we could free ourselves. The problem was getting out and staying out. Thinking of our job as a trap reflects our defenselessness that we learned over the years in letting our jobs provide our sense of security rather than developing these attributes within ourselves.

In what ways are you or did you create your own trap? For example, my statement of self-entrapment was that I expected my employer to provide my security. I relied on my job, my title and my salary to feel good about myself. Once you write how you create your own trap, write down your freedom statement. For example, my freedom statement regarding job security is "security comes from within myself; it is not within my job or in any job." Another example is that titles and salaries do not define who I am as a person. Write down your statements of self-entrapment and statements of freedom. You may choose to include your freedom statements in your daily meditation or as part of your daily affirmations.

Statement of Self-entrapment:

Statement of Freedom:

_____

Statement of Self-entrapment:

_____

Statement of Freedom:

_____

Statement of Self-entrapment:

_____

Statement of Freedom:

_____

The goal of this exercise is to see that we are free to leave our jobs if we desire. We may come to realize that we've created our own trap and, if that is the case, we can free ourselves by taking the responsibility back.

I am free to live the life I desire.

Leaving Our Comfort Zones

I am stuck. This is the 2nd time I tried to leave my job and couldn't. I am so uncomfortable I can't stand it. This time I am going to practice being uncomfortable by doing new things on a regular basis.

I believe that one of the reasons it took me three years and three attempts to leave my job was that I did not practice leaving my comfort zone. I did not know I needed to. We can practice getting out of our comfort zone in many areas of our lives to prepare us for the transition into entrepreneurship.

Now more than ever you need to practice getting out of your comfort zone on a daily basis so your body and mind do not go into "mental shock" from leaving your job. Similar to Challenge I when you were building courage, this exercise helps you continue to expand yourself by having faith in your ability to step outside your comfort zone.

Create a list of things that make you feel comfortable, or things that you do without thinking much about them. For example, you may drive the same way to work every day without even thinking about it.

1. _____

2. _____

3. _____

4. _____

5. _____

6. _____

7. _____

8. _____

9. _____

10. _____

Now that you've created a list of what is comfortable, decide which of the items you would be willing to do differently. Take driving to work, for example. You may choose to expand your comfort zone in this area by driving home different ways that are not familiar to you. Creating a new way home per se. Write down the things that you will begin to do differently to expand your comfort zone.

1. _____

2. _____

3. _____

4. _____

5. _____

6. _____

7. _____

8. _____

9. _____

10. _____

Look back over the list you created above and practice getting out of at least one comfort zone per day until it feels comfortable. For example, if you always drive home from work the same way, drive home as many different ways as you can until you are comfortable with being out of your comfort zone. Then, move on to the next item on the list and do the same. Allow this exercise to take as long as it takes.

I continually work to expand my comfort zone. That way I am mentally prepared when I am asked to do something that scares me, such as speaking to a large group or providing a new service in my business. This exercise keeps me in mental shape.

The goal of this exercise is to help you develop faith in your ability to be comfortable outside your comfort zone – to get used to and familiar with leaving the comfort zone on a regular basis. You may even discover a new comfort zone. Describe any new experiences that came out of expanding your comfort zone.

1. _____

2. _____

3. _____

4. _____

5. _____

I am willing to expand my comfort zone.

Thawing Out

I feel horrible right now. I don't understand it. I left my job and am free now to do what I choose and it doesn't feel good. It's during times like these that I need to remember – just feel the feeling, do what needs to be done and it will pass.

When we have enough faith to let go of our jobs and make a decision not to return, we begin to experience the "thawing out" phase. During this phase, we literally thaw out. We start to feel feelings that we may not have felt before. We experience a deeper level of our feelings, dreams and desires. Thawing out is a homecoming of sorts, meaning that we come home to ourselves. If we do not allow ourselves to go through this phase, we risk the chance of sabotaging our entrepreneurial efforts and returning to a job.

The challenging part of thawing out is that it can be difficult emotionally, mentally, physically and spiritually. The parts of us that we kept dormant and that we had not dealt with yet come back to life during the "thawing out" phase to be healed. Only this time, we make the choice to face whatever challenges are within us for the sake of our business. I saw this happen with many clients and experienced it myself. When I began to thaw out from my job, I was aware of how inadequate I felt in certain social situations. It was an uncomfortable feeling. I recognized that I felt this way as a child and now as an adult, I was dealing with it again. I hated feeling inadequate but I hadn't dealt with this feeling until now. I discovered that one of the reasons I accepted positions in companies was so that I could "fit in" socially and deny the feelings of inadequacy. It worked, but only like a bandage. As an entrepreneur, I chose to face these feelings by talking about them, writing about them, feeling them, accepting them and working through them until they did not have a role in my life anymore.

Another aspect of my thawing out phase was sleeping. During the first year after I left my job, I worked part-time as a consultant and took a nap on many afternoons. I had never taken naps as an adult, never had the luxury before. Once I left my job, I had the time and I needed the sleep.

Annette's experience with thawing out was different. Annette was an administrative assistant for the president of a prestigious bank and one day, when I called the bank to speak with the president, she said, "Oh, honey it's been nice talking to you but as of tomorrow I am leaving this job." I said, curious to know how she could do the one thing that scared me to death, "What are you going to do?" She said, "I do not know but I know one thing, I am not going to be doing this job or any job like this

206

anymore. I think I am going to be a doula." (A doula is a woman who assists women during labor and after childbirth.)

I was so impressed that she could just leave her job and walk into uncertainty that three months later, when I was ready to leave my job, I called her to see how she was doing. She was thawing out. She shared how depressed she had been that she hadn't found any work yet. She shared that she was running out of money and felt suicidal at times. I thought, "So, that's what I have to look forward to. No wonder I'm afraid of leaving my job." We scheduled a time to meet and had a strong spiritual bond. We stayed in touch via e-mail and telephone and then met again the following year. When we met the following year, Annette looked completely different. Her thawing out phase had ended. Her depression lifted and she had lost a considerable amount of weight. And she shared how happy she was now in her life and how good things were going for her.

Thawing out takes time. Do not expect to rush through this phase. We learn a lot about ourselves while we thaw out. We decide what we like and do not like about our lives and ourselves and we seek ways to improve ourselves.

Do the following exercise when you leave your job and return to it as needed.

What feelings have you become aware of now that you have left your job? For example, are you aware of feeling scared, excited, depressed, sick, tired?

_____

_____

How is the thawing out phase affecting you and how are you dealing with each mental, emotional, physical or spiritual challenge? For example, if you are more tired than usual, are you getting enough rest or are you ignoring that you are tired? If you are more depressed than usual, are you doing things like eating healthy, exercising and discussing your depression with your doctor or are you ignoring that you are feeling depressed? Write down how thawing out is affecting you. Then write down what actions you are taking to deal with these effects.

Effects of thawing out:

_____

_____

_____

_____

Actions to deal with this physical, emotional, mental or spiritual condition:

_____

_____

_____

_____

If you are not having any challenges in dealing with thawing out, have you become aware of new behaviors that may be showing up to compensate or deal with pushing away the thawing out phase? These behaviors can include overeating, smoking or drinking more. It can even show up in what appear as healthy ways, such as exercising excessively. Whatever it is, we usually can look at changes in our behaviors to indicate if we are or are not dealing with the thawing out phase. Write down any changes in your behavior.

_____

_____

_____

| *Thawing out is temporary and important.* |

Feelings of Discomfort

Is this process comfortable? Absolutely not. Sometimes, it feels just plain horrible – but it's empowering as hell. I stretched myself today. I feel this anxiety – the pull to stay comfortable and the pull to change. I am working through these feelings.

A common feeling during the thawing out phase is discomfort. We feel uncomfortable – not all of the time, but at times when we might least expect it. Typically we will feel discomfort when we have the greatest opportunity for growth. I used to have panic attacks and even when the panic attacks subsided, the fear of having them was still there. This was especially true when I was thawing out. I remember walking up the stairs to a client's office wondering if I was going to be OK. I just kept walking through these feelings of discomfort until I learned how to be "comfortably uncomfortable."

I learned how to be comfortably uncomfortable by doing what needed to be done even though I felt uncomfortable. I had and continue to have many lessons in feeling comfortably uncomfortable. Feelings of discomfort are just feelings – accept them as part of you. You don't have to like them. I certainly did not like feeling panic. However, it wasn't until I accepted these feelings, talked about them and wrote about and walked through them that they lost their power over me.

Feelings of discomfort become powerful and make decisions for us when we fear them, do not acknowledge them and do not accept them as part of us. Feelings of discomfort can hinder our thawing out process and our business progress if we do not work through them. Take Lisa, for example. She felt discomfort about initiating a meeting with a retail storeowner who operated a business just three doors down from her office. She saw an opportunity for the two businesses to explore a strategic alliance. She wasn't able to move through the feelings of discomfort and introduce herself to this storeowner. Unfortunately, the more time that went by, the stronger the feelings of discomfort became. She shared with me that the reason she hadn't introduced herself to him is that she heard he is not a nice person. She was allowing her feelings of discomfort to make decisions for her. The discomfort does not go away until we work through it and take whatever action we need to take. Lisa decided not to contact this retail storeowner. Even if she worked through her discomfort, introduced herself to the storeowner and decided that an alliance was not an option, at least she would have had the benefit of working through the discomfort.

Can you let yourself feel comfortably uncomfortable, meaning feeling the discomfort and doing what needs to be done anyway? Many times we are intimidated by feelings of discomfort and let these feeling hold us back from making progress in our personal and professional lives. The benefit of feeling discomfort and doing what needs to be done anyway is that when we grow through our discomfort, our business grows, too. Name three situations that you feel uncomfortable about and what you need to do despite your discomfort. Then put a date when you will take this specific action.

The goal of this exercise is to feel the discomfort, work through it and learn the skill of being comfortably uncomfortable.

Situations you feel uncomfortable about:

1. _____

_____

_____

2. _____

_____

_____

3. _____

_____

_____

Now write down the actions you will take to confront your discomfort and your accountability date. For example, if you were given a business lead to a potential client and feel uncomfortable about calling, the actions might include making a call to the potential customer, setting up an appointment and meeting in person.

	Actions	**Accountability Date**
1.	_____	_____
2.	_____	_____
3.	_____	_____

4. _____ _____

5. _____ _____

6. _____ _____

7. _____ _____

8. _____ _____

9. _____ _____

10. _____ _____

What did you learn about yourself from having taken action on situations that felt uncomfortable? For example, I learned from recognizing my discomfort and doing what needed to be done that the strongest feelings of discomfort are present when I have the greatest opportunity for personal or professional growth.

_____

_____

_____

_____

_____

_____

I can be comfortably uncomfortable.

No, You Are Not Crazy

For some stupid reason, I fear falling apart. I fear somehow that the job and money keep me glued there – as if I am not whole. I fear being not OK. I fear feeling crazy – like I don't fit. The decision I'm making doesn't fit. I'm going out on my own. I fear the change and how it's going to affect me. I fear the anticipation of what's on the other side. Will I be OK?

Transitioning out of an employee mentality can be emotionally challenging. It was the most difficult transition of my life. My thoughts about "being crazy" came up while I was still employed. It took me a year of professional counseling and two prior years of denying my entrepreneurial feelings to become aware of my desire to be an entrepreneur and to be OK with it. What surprised me about counseling was that I went for issues that had nothing to do (or so I thought) with wanting to become an entrepreneur, and found out eight months later that I wanted to quit my job.

Some of the clients I counseled have expressed concern that they have wondered if they were going crazy for making or having made this transition into entrepreneurship. Cindy spent fourteen years as a librarian before she was laid off and decided to become an entrepreneur. One day during a business counseling session, she said to me, "Suzanne, I know you are not a psychologist, but sometimes I feel like I am going crazy." I looked at her and said, "Many clients tell me the same thing so it must be normal. I, too, went through these feelings of going crazy. So no, you are not alone in feeling these feelings."

Clients would be calmed to know that they were not alone in having these feelings as well as other feelings that arose in the thawing out phase. These feelings pass. The best way that I and many of my clients got through them was to develop faith and belief in ourselves. We also needed to practice balanced living – taking care of ourselves mentally, physically, spiritually and emotionally each and every day.

How have you found it emotionally challenging in making the transition from an employee mentality? For example, have you had feelings of being or going crazy surface? Are you accepting your feelings or pushing them away? One way to accept your feelings is to just feel them, to talk about them with supportive people and to write about them. Trying not to think about them and not talking about them will not make them go away. I tried that for many years and it did not work. Our feelings are there for us to feel and recognize.

I am OK. This, too, shall pass.

Feeling "Icky, Strange or Weird"

I'm starting to feel the effects of having left my job. I feel strange, weird in a way. That old icky feeling of change is starting to affect me. Oh, I do not like these feelings. I wish they would just go away. I know... I know... that the only way they go away is for me to feel them.

Feeling icky, strange or weird are normal feelings. They come about in the thawing out phase – when we are transitioning out of our job. These feelings are usually the most evident when it is obvious to the outside world that we have transitioned in some way. Feeling icky, strange or weird can happen at any stage of our professional growth when we outgrow our prior comfort zone. For example, I felt these uncomfortable feelings when I was promoted into a more responsible and more visible position within a company. I also felt these feelings when I left my job and no longer had a title, salary or office.

Think of the statement "getting comfortable in our new skin." That is exactly what we are doing – learning to get comfortable in our new life as an entrepreneur. Leaving our jobs is the outward sign that we are making progress. We may have seen many changes within ourselves by working through the previous challenges but now it is evident to not only us but to the world that we are making changes.

Feeling icky, strange or weird is temporary. It will not last forever. Lisa expressed that she felt icky and wasn't sure how to describe the feeling. This feeling came up after she experienced tremendous personal growth through business counseling, had made many changes in her personal and professional life and was now experiencing the effects of those changes. These effects included relocating into a larger and more prominent office space and dealing with more prominent business people. She shared that she didn't feel like the new store was hers – that it didn't feel real to her yet.

These icky feelings surface at a moment when you professionally achieve a higher level of status than you are comfortable with. I recall helping a business college get sponsors for an event. I did this as a favor to the college. The college rewarded me by making me a sponsor. When I walked into the event, my company's name was at the center of one of the guest tables. I felt strange and weird. I felt like I didn't belong there and yet I knew it was where I was meant to be. I hadn't yet grown into my "new shoes."

Have you felt icky, strange or weird feelings since your transition into entrepreneurship? If so, describe those feelings. Did they surprise you? Were they new feelings or have you felt them before? If you've felt them before, what were the circumstances? The goal of this exercise is to recognize, admit and accept your icky, strange or weird feelings and do what needs to be done anyway. Describe any icky, strange or weird feelings that may have come up for you.

_____

_____

_____

Can you identify when you first felt the icky, strange or weird feeling you described above? I am referring to the first time, meaning it may not have been when you transitioned out of your job or started the business. It may go back to childhood or sometime in your teenage years. The icky feeling you have now may relate to a feeling you had in childhood. If you can get to the source, write about it. You may not have to go through this experience again.

_____

_____

_____

All my feelings are valid.

Feeling Insecure

For some stupid reason – I feel insecure. I hate that feeling. Sometimes I feel like this feeling is written all over my face.

Feelings of insecurity are common when we are in transition or feel the threat of a transition. It is my experience that we may compromise ourselves if we do not deal with our insecure feelings. I compromised myself as an employee by giving more of myself to my work than expected and working many hours over my salaried 40-hour job. Judy was having this experience of compromising herself as an entrepreneur. Judy walked in to a meeting with the goal of getting a sponsor for her radio show. She left the meeting being a contractor for this company. She settled for something she didn't even anticipate. Somehow she thought she needed the offer this company was making her.

Several months after this arrangement, Judy became aware that she compromised herself because of her insecurity. She asked me, "Why is that? Why would I walk in there and anticipate getting a sponsor and leave with an agreement to do work for this company?" She answered her own question. When feelings of insecurity come up, she compromises herself to feel secure.

How are your feelings of insecurity revealed? Are there any behaviors that you say, "What did I do that for?" that might trigger a deeper feeling of insecurity?

_____

_____

_____

How can you accept your feelings of insecurity without compromising yourself? Can you stand up for what you believe and know is right for you? How will you do this?

_____

_____

_____

I am safe and secure within myself.

Feeling Inadequate

I felt so inadequate today. I went to an event that I was invited to go to and wanted to attend. And while I was there I felt inadequate – like I didn't belong there. I hate this feeling.

One of the most challenging feelings for me to deal with when I was transitioning out of my job was the feeling of inadequacy – that feeling that somehow I'm just not right, just don't quite fit in. Once we accept – instead of deny or push away – our feelings of inadequacy, they lose their power over us. Although I experienced more feelings of inadequacy as an employee than I did as an entrepreneur, the inadequacy feelings I experienced as an entrepreneur were more vivid. They were stronger and got my attention so I could face them and ask the question, "Why am I feeling these feelings?" While all feelings are valid, I learned to examine my feelings of inadequacy and saw that some of my thoughts about myself were distorted. What I discovered was that I was trying to "fit in" – be like everyone else. I worked through these feelings of inadequacy by having faith in my uniqueness – in being who I really was.

When do the feelings of inadequacy come to the surface? Is it when you walk into a room full of people? Is it when you learning something new?

_____

_____

_____

_____

What are you learning about yourself as you face your feelings of inadequacy? What are these feelings telling you? Are they telling you that you need to accept yourself just as you are? Are they telling you that you need to love yourself? Are they telling you that when you are tired and over-extend yourself that you are more prone to feelings of inadequacy? Write down what these feelings are telling you.

_____

_____

_____

_____

_____

_____

I accept myself exactly as I am.

Feeling Vulnerable

I feel vulnerable, so very vulnerable. This feeling is so strong – it makes me want to turn back and forget about this entrepreneurial venture. But why would I give up the very thing I want?

Feeling vulnerable is a big challenge for entrepreneurs. Here we gathered all that strength to leave our jobs and now we feel vulnerable. It doesn't make sense. Or does it? There is a benefit to feeling vulnerable. It is the awareness and acceptance of our reliance on ourselves. We become aware that our security lies within us, not outside of us. When we feel vulnerable, we have released our dependence on things, such as our jobs that were not giving us the security we desired in our lives anyway.

During the early phases of entrepreneurship, I felt vulnerable. This feeling did not feel good to me. I thought, "What am I doing? I know I want to make this change but it feels horrible right now." I shared this with a client who was also feeling challenged by his feelings of vulnerability. He felt weak for feeling so vulnerable and had a difficult time dealing with it. I shared with him that entrepreneurship is for the brave. It is for those of us willing to have faith in ourselves and experience our lives in a new way. Here he had been thinking that he was weak because he was feeling so vulnerable and I tell him he was brave.

The irony of feeling vulnerable and many of the other uncomfortable feelings transitioning into entrepreneurship is that we may not feel these feelings until we let go of our jobs and recognize our self-reliance. I recall going to several holiday parties the month after I left my job and feeling extremely vulnerable. I began to question why I left my job. I realized at these parties that my whole social persona had changed because I no longer had a boss to talk about, co-workers or any work situation to socially discuss. It didn't feel very good.

Feeling vulnerable is an important part of the experience of becoming an entrepreneur. Our feelings of vulnerability help us develop our faith in ourselves.

Describe your feelings of vulnerability. Under what situation did these feelings come up? What does this feeling feel like to you? For example, does it feel scary, uncomfortable or is it more of a feeling of awareness?

_____

_____

_____

_____

What are your feelings of vulnerability teaching you about yourself? For example, I learned that a big part of my social skill set was to talk about my job. Now that I didn't have a job, I needed to learn to develop myself so I could comfortably talk about me – my hobbies, my business and my vision for my future.

| Feelings of vulnerability teach me about me. |

Feeling Desperate

Here I am again, feeling desperate - like I'm not going to "make it." I worked through this feeling before – so I am sure I can do it again.

Rose Lee came in for business counseling because she felt desperate. While her feelings of desperation made her seek help, they also hindered her from accomplishing what she desired. Her funding had been cut for the production of her television talk show. Prior to the funding being cut, her show was taped and aired through the same station. Now the station was only going to air her show, not tape or edit it. She needed to find someone to provide the technical production of the show and funding to pay for it. She felt desperate, sounded desperate and acted desperate. Her feelings of desperation were actually perpetuating the situation she was trying to get out of.

So how did she get funded and locate a new technical producer for her show? It wasn't by feeling or acting desperate. She worked on developing her faith in herself and in the mission of her television show and learned skills that would help her locate funding and a technical producer. She then took action that reflected this faith in herself. In her desperation, she made many calls that did not give her the results she needed. When she developed faith in herself, she got clarity about what she needed to do. She contacted the television producer of the county's public television station and was given a grant to tape her show for an entire season. Not only did the county tape and edit her show, it also aired her show on the county channel. As a result of working through her desperation and having faith in herself, her show was being aired on the county channel and well as the network it originally aired on.

How can we feel desperate and then let go of our desperation so we can be positive in our business? The answer is to look inside and see why we feel desperate. Where does this feeling come from? What does it tell us? When we feel desperate, we are questioning ourselves – not having faith in ourselves. Our feelings of desperation are a reflection of our faith in ourselves. What do you need to learn from these feelings? Our feelings sometimes tell us things that we do not want to know but need to know.

Are you feeling desperate? What do these feelings relate to? Desperation for money? Desperation for power? Feel and then describe these feelings. How are these feelings helping or hurting you? For example, Rose Lee's feelings of desperation helped her seek out business counseling. They also hindered her in that she sounded desperate and acted desperate when she was trying to locate funding.

_____

_____

I have faith in myself.

LEAVING THE COMFORT ZONE
CHALLENGE REVIEW

One of the main goals of the Leaving The Comfort Zone challenge is to recognize that the transition into entrepreneurship can be uncomfortable. We may be challenged in ways that we have never been challenged before. Know that anytime we leave what we know and what is familiar to us we will experience some of these feelings. We can learn to feel the discomfort and do what needs to be done anyway. We can expect to feel an array of feelings as we leave our comfort zones. The important part of this challenge is to develop faith in ourselves and accept and work through the feelings we are experiencing. Give yourself as much time as you need to work through this time of transition.

What did you learn about yourself that you didn't know or want to acknowledge before? For example, I learned that I was seeking security outside of myself. I learned my feelings were teaching me things about myself that I didn't know or didn't want to know.

_____

_____

_____

_____

_____

_____

How do you acknowledge your uncomfortable feelings? Do you write about them? Talk about them? Know that expressing these uncomfortable feelings is the first step to lessening their hold on you. Write down how you acknowledge these feelings.

_____

_____

_____

_____

_____

How did this exercise help you build faith in yourself? Did your feelings of desperation help you seek guidance and direction? Did your feelings of insecurity help you realize that you can choose to be secure within yourself?

_____

_____

_____

_____

_____

What was the most difficult part of this challenge for you? For me it was learning to deal with uncertainty and to realize that I would be OK without the security of a job. I learned that the security I desired was inside of me.

In actual life every great enterprise begins with and takes its first forward step in faith.

August Von Schlegel

CHALLENGE VII
BEFORE THE MONEY FLOWS

In my pursuit of money and success, I discovered something even more powerful – the ability to trust myself and to trust my entrepreneurial journey. With this trust, I have something all the money in the world can't buy.

It wasn't until I became an entrepreneur that I realized how money and success were tightly bound within myself. I began to realize that when I made money, I felt great, and when I didn't make money, I felt terrible.

I struggled with the correlation of success and money. How could I feel successful all the time instead of just when I made money? Because there were so many times when I was not making money and feeling terrible, I forced myself to evaluate my understanding of success. What did success really mean to me? How could I feel successful all the time? I needed to find out.

I soon discovered that I did not trust the process of success. I did not understand what success really meant to me. It was during this critical time before the money flowed that I learned how to trust and feel successful. Success was within me – not outside me. Had money flowed to me during this critical time of redefining my understanding of success and learning how to trust, I never would have truly experienced success nor would I have learned how to trust the process that I was in. I would still be experiencing the yo-yo effect of success – allowing my success to be determined by how much money I earned. I needed to learn to trust the process and understand what success really meant to me.

My definition of success defines what is important to me, not what is important to the outside world. I now believe that I am successful because I live the life I desire. This definition is unconditional – meaning that it doesn't change if I make a lot of money or a little money. It is a standard for me to live by.

It has taken me several years to learn how to trust the process and live by my new definition of success. I realize now that in this process of redefining success, I expanded my knowledge, trust and belief in myself. I learned what was important to me.

The time before the money flows is perhaps the most important time in entrepreneurship. It is when we "crystallize" ourselves – we become what we believe – through the act of entrepreneurship. It is during this time that we truly know we are on the path, that we are on the way to entrepreneurial success. Why? Because we have become successful within ourselves. We are no longer filled with doubt but rather filled with self-knowledge and a belief in what we are doing that is beyond even our own comprehension. You may ask entrepreneurs who have re-evaluated their definition of success and who trust the process but have not yet experienced the flow of money, "Why are you doing this?" If they have created a definition of success that is a part of who they are and truly trust the process, they will answer with a powerful statement that is basically summed up in two words: "I believe." "I believe it is what I am meant to be doing." They are armed with knowledge – of themselves. They trust the process and have moved into a new level of living, thinking and believing. Their response will completely affirm who they are. They trust that the money will flow rather than question when it will flow. This is the value in getting through the time "before the money flows."

**Just trust yourself.
Then you will know how to live.**

Johann Wolfgang von Goethe

Trusting Yourself and the Process

The answer is to trust myself and trust the process. I tried trusting money, that didn't work. I tried trusting success, that didn't work either. I need to trust myself and the process before either money or success can come to me.

Trust is at the core of experiencing the success we desire. This core or foundation is built on trusting ourselves and trusting the process. The pace of our progress, especially before the money flows, depends on developing this level of trust in ourselves and in the overall process – in the overall order of things. You may ask, "How do I simply trust the process when I don't know where I am going?" The answer is to know and trust that wherever you are being led is for your highest good. When we believe that what is happening in our lives is for our highest good, we can trust ourselves and trust the process.

Trusting can be difficult. In order to trust, we need to let go of control. We need to let go of the way we think things are supposed to work out. We usually don't think that we need to let go of control until we have reached a point in our lives when our way, the way we think things should be, doesn't work. It is at this point that we have a choice. We can either let go of control and start trusting or we can try to control our lives even more. We may try to control our lives more by working more, working harder or forcing a solution to a problem. I chose to control and probably suffered mental strain unnecessarily because I didn't want to let go of control. Letting go of control and learning to trust myself and the process was extremely difficult for me. But I did it, not because I wanted to, but because my way wasn't working. It wasn't creating the results I desired in my life. It took me a long time to let go of control and trust.

Most clients who were challenged financially, mentally or on some other level, came in for business counseling either because they, too, needed to let go of control or because they stopped trusting. Their way wasn't working. They got scared, which is a normal response when our way isn't working or we stop trusting. The problem is that when we stop trusting, we stop moving forward. Everything in our lives, including the money that we want to flow to us, is on "hold." Money cannot flow to us when we do not trust that it will flow to us. We need to work through whatever feeling or emotion stopped us from trusting in the first place and begin trusting again.

How do we learn to trust? We learn to trust by making the decision to trust. Lack of trust is why most people choose not to make the journey into entrepreneurship, or to turn back and not complete the journey. We choose to trust ourselves and the process. We then take appropriate actions that reflect that trust. Several years ago, I knew it was time to let go of my office space, move back to my home office and accept a long-term contract with the Small Business Development Center to counsel clients. I didn't understand "why" I needed to do this; I just knew and trusted that it was what I needed to do. I took action that reflected this trust by moving out of my office space and accepting the contract. I knew it was right for me, even though I could not justify it and could not completely explain or understand it. I just trusted it. Years later, I understand the role that contract had in my life. It gave me the experience to write this book. We learn to trust.

Once we begin to trust ourselves, we can begin to trust the process and the journey we are on. When we trust ourselves, we trust the process.

Another way to trust is to realize that we've earned the right to trust. We earn trust when we give ourselves credit for the work we've done to get to this point in our personal and professional lives. We didn't get here by accident. We worked on ourselves to get here. We became brave, we learned to listen to ourselves, to change, develop our uniqueness, persevere, strengthen ourselves and have faith. We earned the right to trust.

The same principles apply in learning to trust ourselves and the process as in maintaining this level of trust. We can increase our trust by respecting and acknowledging ourselves and recognizing our value as a person. Once we maintain a level of trust in ourselves and in the process, we need to continue to grow personally and professionally. We do this by continuing to improve ourselves and letting go of whatever is not working in our lives.

Are you trying to control the process or do you trust the process? One way to know if you are controlling or trusting is by examining your thoughts and feelings. For example, when I am trying to control the process I get uptight, start worrying and feel fearful about my future. When I trust the process I feel focused, enjoy each day and feel positive about my future.

_____

_____

_____

_____

Are you willing to let go of control and trust the process? What do you need to let go of so you can start trusting? For example, I needed to let go of controlling the way I wanted my future to unfold and learn to trust that it would unfold for my highest good. Describe what you need to let go of so you can start trusting.

_____

_____

_____

_____

_____

Learning to trust takes time. As you begin to trust yourself and the process, describe what it feels like to trust. Just like you experienced discomfort by trying new things and experiencing new feelings by working through challenges in this book, this feeling of trust may not be comfortable at first. Expect that. If it is uncomfortable or different, you are growing and experiencing trust. Describe what it feels like to trust.

_____

_____

_____

_____

_____

_____

If you are having a difficult time learning to trust, write about it in your journal every day for a week. Ask yourself, "Why is it so difficult for me to trust?" and wait for the answer. You can discover more of yourself and find out why you do not trust. It took me a long time and a lot of writing to learn to trust the process.

We can increase our level of trust by acknowledging ourselves for the progress we've made. For example, I worked at developing my trust in myself and in the process by accepting compliments from others, treating myself as I would like others to treat me and knowing that I was living my life to its fullest. In what ways will you acknowledge yourself for the progress you've made on this journey thus far? You can continue to increase this trust in yourself by doing this exercise regularly.

_____

_____

_____

_____

_____

Sometimes we forget everything we've learned and stop trusting. In this case, we need to go back to basics and find ways to help us trust the process. For example, it helps me remember to trust when I immerse myself in nature and reflect on the natural order of things in the universe – how birds, fish and animals instinctively know how to live and find food, how a spider makes a web and trusts that his creation will provide him food. What will you do to remember to trust when you've forgotten?

_____

_____

_____

_____

_____

I trust myself and I trust the process.

Being in the Flow

Every day I am amazed with the knowledge that I come away with. I really learn something new every day.

Once we learn to trust, we enter a new experience; being in the flow. When we are in the flow, things work for us. Everything we need shows up exactly when we need it – ideas, people and money. Situations happen and unfold naturally. We trust that situations will turn out for our highest good. We do not have to force results or outcomes – they happen in their own time. Our responsibility is to continue trusting ourselves, trusting the process and staying in the flow.

The challenge of staying in the flow is that things may not happen when we expect them to. We get out of the flow when we get scared, panic or worry that things will be OK. It may feel unnatural to stay in the flow and not worry about today, tomorrow or the future, especially before the money flows. This is when we are most challenged to stay in the flow. The more we trust the process, the easier it is to stay in the flow.

Sometimes, the flow will become so comfortable that we question ourselves. "Is it really OK that I am not worried about this?" Or "Shouldn't I be worrying about money?" "Is it OK to just be OK even though my financial situation is tight right now?" I caught myself asking these questions many times before I got used to being in and trusting the flow. They were no longer questions of worry, however. They were confirmations that I was experiencing the flow even though I wasn't used to it.

When we are in the flow, we trust instead of judge. We give up being the "judge" – judging that we have enough or do not have enough, judging that we need more than we have, judging that we are or are not OK in our current circumstance. It is in trusting that we stay in the flow; it is in judging that we risk leaving the flow. The choice is ours now – to stay in the flow or not to stay in the flow – and we make that choice by trusting or not trusting the time before the money flows.

When is it difficult for you to stay in the flow? For example, it is difficult for me to stay in the flow when I feel challenged financially. It is also difficult for me to stay in the flow when I do not have any pending contracts or new work in sight.

_____

_____

_____

_____

_____

How will you stay in the flow when you are challenged by the situations you described above? For example, I consciously maintain my mental, emotional, physical and spiritual stamina by making sure I get to the gym regularly, do my daily meditations, pray, consciously decide to trust the process and myself, read my affirmations and talk with supportive friends.

_____

_____

_____

How will you recognize you are out of the flow? For example, when I get out of the flow I experience physical symptoms such as heart palpitations. I start feeling a lot of fear, wake up at night, start to worry about the future and stop taking care of my basic needs such as eating right and taking time for fun. I get very serious and lose my spontaneity.

_____

_____

_____

_____

When you get out of the flow, what will you do to get back in it? For example, before I can get back in the flow, I first have to become aware that I am out of the flow, and then I can take action. I start with the basics; making sure I am eating healthy foods and taking time to eat, making sure I get enough sleep by going to bed at a reasonable hour, consciously engaging in daily prayer and meditation, and spending time reading my affirmations and writing in my journal.

_____

_____

_____

_____

The goal of this exercise is to see the importance of getting in and staying in the flow and being aware of what you need to do to get back in the flow.

I live in the flow – the flow is comfortable for me.

You Are Exactly Where You Need to Be

I feel a deep sense of knowing that I am where I need to be. I am further than I ever thought or imagined in my life. Maybe it wasn't about the money.

Trusting that we are where we are meant to be helps us deal with the time before the money flows. It helps us move forward. Trusting that we are where we need to be on every level – emotionally, mentally, physically and spiritually – is a form of acceptance. When we accept, we move forward. Even if we do not like where we are on our journey but trust that we are where we are meant to be, we still move forward.

"You are exactly where you need to be" can be a difficult concept to understand, especially if we want to be somewhere else in our lives. Oftentimes I hear clients say, "I'm almost there." Many times we put our lives, or part of our lives, "on hold" to try to be somewhere we are not. Once we begin to understand that we are exactly where we need to be, the pressure to be or do something different is removed. We no longer waste our energy asking questions such as, "Why do I have to deal with this?" "How long do I have to wait?"

When we trust that we are exactly where we need to be we open ourselves to experiences along our entrepreneurial journey.

How can you acknowledge that you are right where you need to be for today? What lesson might you be learning that is important?

I am right where I need to be.

Intuition – Using Our "Knower"

*I am at this "place" intuitively but not yet in the physical world.
It's like I know I'm there – I just cannot see it yet and I don't
know what it looks like.*

Intuition is something that everyone has but not everyone uses. Our intuition is often subtle and soft. It doesn't yell at us to get our attention. Sometimes we don't like what our intuition tells us and so we don't pay attention to it; other times we block it out all together. If we trust our intuition and follow it, we move forward.

There are two steps to using our intuition to our advantage. The first step is hearing what our intuition has to say. We become consciously aware of what is being spoken to us and through us when we hear our intuition. The second step is to trust our intuition by taking appropriate action. This is often where most people choose not to use their intuition to their advantage and instead follow their will. Unfortunately, when we do not trust our intuition, we miss an opportunity to move forward in our entrepreneurial journey.

Sometimes our intuition tries to get our attention and we just don't want to hear it. My intuition has told me many things in my personal and professional life – to quit my job and go back to school, to accept certain jobs, to turn down other jobs, to work with some people and not work with others. Did I pay attention to everything my intuition told me? Not always. Why wouldn't I pay attention to my intuition? Because my will got in the way. I wanted to do things my way, not how my intuition suggested. The one situation that finally got my attention was when I got lost scuba diving at night in the Florida Keys. I was diving with a friend and trusted her instead of trusting my intuition, which was telling me to surface and see where I was. I didn't pay attention. I stayed underwater and when I did finally surface, we were far from the boat. We almost were left out there for the night because the boat captain thought we were lost or got picked up by another boat. Scary. That's what it took for me to hear and pay attention to my intuition.

I have worked with clients who shared that while everything looked right for a deal they were making, it didn't feel right. My suggestion has always been to trust their intuition. In the situations where clients have said they knew it didn't feel right but they didn't pay attention, they were usually sorry. Abby, an inventor, had a situation where her intuition said "no" but she said "yes" and proceeded with a contract. She later shared with me, "I knew this didn't feel right but I did it anyway." Abby was right. The contract turned bad.

We can enhance the use of our intuition by practicing a balanced lifestyle, spending time in nature, respecting our feelings, meditating, trusting ourselves and trusting the process. The more we trust and act on our intuition, the more intuition we will have. Intuition works the other way as well, meaning the less we trust it and take appropriate action, the less intuition we will have.

Describe a situation where you heard and acted on your intuition. Use the examples described above to stimulate your memory.

_____

_____

_____

_____

_____

_____

Describe a situation where you did not pay attention to or believe your intuition, later learning that your intuition was correct?

Similar to the example that I gave with regard to not paying attention to my intuition while I was diving and got lost in the night.

_____

_____

_____

The goal of this exercise is to pay attention to, trust and act on your intuition. The more we become aware of the role it has played in our life, the easier it will be for us to pay attention to our intuition in the future.

I trust my intuition.

Watch for Coincidences

Amazing things continue to happen. My next client "appeared" as all the previous ones had.

Coincidences are signs – indicators – that we are either on the right path or need to change paths. Coincidences are situations that get our attention and can sometimes happen mysteriously. We do not always understand how and why a coincidence happens. Coincidences include all kinds of life situations such as running into someone you've been meaning to contact, getting a call from someone you've been thinking of or having someone show up in your life with a solution to a problem.

The challenge with coincidences, like intuition, is that although they have our highest good or our best interests in mind, we may not like what they tell us and so we choose to ignore them. Diana had the strange coincidence of breaking her ankle after a series of experiences that were telling her to slow down.

This resulted in her being bedridden for weeks. This coincidence, Diana believes, happened because she ignored the other signs her body gave her to slow down her lifestyle. She laughed when she told me that she couldn't believe that it took breaking her ankle before she would slow down. She got the message that the coincidence of breaking her ankle was trying to tell her. She respected the message by slowing down her lifestyle.

I watch for coincidences to see if clients are on their path or not. If they are on their path, situations will happen that will let them know that they are going in the right direction. One way I always knew clients were on their path was when they would start our business counseling session with excitement and say, "Suzanne, you are just never going to believe what happened … who I met … how I got this deal …" Coincidences that indicate we are on our path are exciting and exhilarating.

Coincidences happen in ways that are often beyond our comprehension. Sometimes we meet people in strange places such as elevators or parking lots – people who are meant to be on our path. Coincidences help us if we let them. Coincidences just seem to work or show up when we need them. For example, Robert, who owns a concrete company, had to let go of two of his best employees because of an issue regarding their citizenship. Revenue dropped dramatically as Robert placed ads in the newspaper to replace these employees. All the while he tried to locate a past employee, Mike, but had lost all contact with him and couldn't locate him. A few days later, Robert went to a pizza restaurant for lunch and Mike was his server. Three days later, Mike was working for Robert.

Describe recent coincidences. What are these coincidences suggesting – that you are on the path or that you need to alter your path? Consider the situations described above to help you recognize what your coincidences are telling you and if you are on the right path or not.

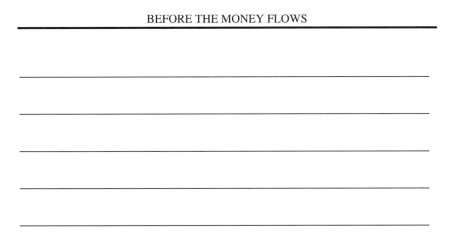

Coincidences help me get on and stay on my path.

Look for Guardian Guides

OK guides, it's your turn. What do you see for me?

Guardian guides are people who show up in your life to help you for no other reason than for the sake of helping. Guardian guides are very subtle. They don't jump out at you and say, "I'm here to help." They gently provide their support in the form of leads, advice, financial assistance or help in some other way. Guardian guides are especially helpful to recognize before the money flows because they validate that you are on your path.

I began to recognize that guardian guides existed and helped clients create their path. Clients would share with me that they had people in their lives who had no affiliation to the business other than to provide assistance or guidance. These guardian guides weren't paid; they just wanted to help.

Claudia's guardian guide was the most obvious one I saw. Claudia shared that a man she had met only once called her to give her business leads. He didn't even have a telephone. He would call her on a pay phone. And his leads were valid. She generated several business alliances and contracts through this guardian guide.

241

Rose Lee had a guardian guide who helped her financially. She had been taking care of Charlie, an older gentleman, for about six months – taking him to church on Sundays, bringing him several meals each week and spending time with him. Charlie was an old friend of her father who had died eighteen months prior and so Charlie was special to her. When she and Charlie spent time together, Rose Lee would talk about her business, how things were going, and how her business was progressing. Charlie died of old age and Rose Lee organized his funeral. She got a call several weeks later from a trust attorney who stated that Charlie had left her a considerable amount of money. Rose Lee was shocked – she saw Charlie as a sign that she was on the right path in her business. Charlie was a guardian guide after all.

Guardian guides help you know you are on your path. They are a part of your path and they show up to help. Who are your guardian guides? Is there anyone in your life who helps you who has no affiliation with the business other than to help? Who supports you emotionally, mentally, spiritually and perhaps financially?

1. _____

2. _____

3. _____

4. _____

5. _____

Are you open to receiving the help that guardian guides provide? If not, why? Sometimes, we are closed off to outside help – wanting to do things our way or not wanting any guidance. Sometimes we create challenges when we do not see the help that is before us. Write down your willingness to receive the help of guardian guides.

_____

_____

_____

_____

_____

I respect and welcome my guardian guides.

Working Through the "In-Between" Phase

I am in this in-between state. It's like I see myself on the bridge between the land and wherever it is I am going. I know I am well into my journey – I have many lessons behind me. Like other phases of my journey, I know this one is important.

The time between when we start a business and when we make a comfortable income from it is called the "in-between" phase. This phase requires a lot of trust so we can move through this phase. When we are "in between," success must take place in our minds, bodies and spirits first. Anything that interferes with our success will show up during this time. For example, if we still have a negative belief that we are not worthy, it will show up. If we still practice perfectionism, it will show up. Our beliefs about money – if they are not helping us – will show up. Whatever it is that hinders the flow of money will be revealed to us during this phase.

We must still have money to live during the in-between phase. Sometimes the money comes from different sources – savings, part-time jobs, lines of credit and other sources that we may not have considered tapping into before or that we were not open to before. Coincidences may also appear that generate hope or help us financially. If we are going in the direction we are meant to be going in, what we need will show up when we need it to help us through this phase. If we are not going in the direction we are meant to be in, opportunities will show up to further guide us. Often, we look at these opportunities to guide us as problems when, in fact, they are solutions.

This concept of seeing problems or challenges as opportunities may be one of the most important and at the same time most difficult concepts to grasp in entrepreneurship. It is a concept that I used to help clients and help myself during the in-between phase. Has everything in my entrepreneurial journey worked out the way I thought or wanted? Absolutely not. However, everything did work out the way it was supposed to work out. One example that I recently reflected on was that had I become financially successful in what I "thought" I was meant to do – provide business consulting to corporations, I may never have written this book. The journey has led me to realize that the in-between phase is an important part of the journey.

I have found it helpful to grasp the "what I need will show up" concept when dealing with the in-between phase. I realize that everything I need will be there when I need it. This is most evident to me when I look in hindsight at my journey thus far. It is in looking back and gaining insight that I move forward. Looking back helps me know and trust that I was on a path all along. I was only alone when I forgot to ask for help, only frightened when I forgot that others were there to support me, only feeling poor when I forgot to look inside myself and not just in my bank account.

I challenge you to allow the journey to unfold and walk through the in-between phase. Just as we cannot force a flower to open or know what color it is before its time, we cannot force the entrepreneurial journey or expect things before their time. Trust the process. Think of yourself as being prepared – purified – like the finest diamonds. Imperfections are being worked out so that we can be clearer about who we are and what we are meant to do. Don't be afraid to ask yourself, "Am I going in the right direction? Does this direction serve my highest good?" Let the answer come to you. Wait for the answer if you have to.

What imperfections are being worked out or need to be worked out in you during this in-between phase? Are you typically negative, impatient or easily frustrated? For example, Alan felt sorry for himself for not being able to get new clients and grow his business. This attitude negatively affected his business and his ability to get through the in-between phase. It wasn't until he began changing his attitude that he began moving through this phase. Describe imperfections you are aware of within yourself that you are willing to work on.

_____

_____

_____

_____

_____

What will you replace these imperfections with to help you move through this phase? For example, Alan became aware that he had a negative attitude toward the future of his business and had to work at becoming optimistic. Once he allowed this new attitude to take root, his business improved and he moved through the in-between phase.

_____

_____

_____

What can you do to help you trust the process while you are moving through the in-between phase? For example, Rose Lee applied for and received numerous awards that helped her trust the process and let her know she was on the right path while she was working through the in-between phase.

_____

_____

_____

_____

This phase takes as long as it needs to take. We cannot rush it – we can only trust it. Write a note to yourself to describe your willingness to trust the in-between phase. Reflect back on what you wrote when you feel like things are not working out or you want to give up.

_____

_____

_____

_____

I am making progress each and every day.

Trust the Ebb and Flow of Money

Tonight, just a few moments ago, I made a vow to never worry or be concerned about money again.

Just as the tides fluctuate naturally, our money situation fluctuates naturally. I had to learn to let money flow to me and from me naturally. Many of my entrepreneurial lessons have been regarding money issues. I did not trust the flow of money nor did I trust money. I was afraid of money because I gave it power over me. So in order to deal with money, I used to hoard it. The more money I saved, the more I felt in control. But actually, the more money I saved, the more I felt enslaved to it. I learned that money is not meant to be hoarded, feared or abused. Money is not meant to have power or be given power to. Money just is.

Money just so happens to be the way our society measures success. This is not a bad thing or a good thing; it is just a fact. Let's face it, we need money to survive and live. The reality is that there is plenty of money. There is neither a lack of money nor an excess of money; there is a perfect balance of money in this world. Our goal is to find our perfect balance of money and trust its ebb and flow.

Some people choose to deal with money from a spiritual perspective in order to learn that money just is and release the power it had over them. If money is given power or it is abused in any way, it will be difficult to let it flow naturally to and from us. I had this challenge – giving power to money. My friend Laura once said to me when I was challenged with money issues, "Money is not my source. God is my source." I thought, "Wow. I never thought of money that way." The way she learned to deal with money was that it did not have any power over her; she did not give it any power.

I used to think that without money I would shrivel up and die, not be able to function in this world or end up homeless. That is because I gave money power over me. That is just not true for me anymore. By learning to accept money for what it is, learning to recognize my skills and my place in this world, and learning to trust the ebb and flow of money, those thoughts that I used to have are no longer valid. It is when I think thoughts like that that I am giving power to money – making money more powerful than I am, more capable than I am. That is just not the truth.

I came to understand that in order for money to flow freely to me, it also needed to flow freely from me. I do not mean by spending lavishly or irresponsibly. I mean by buying what I needed to buy, treating myself well and letting money flow naturally to and from me. This concept of trusting the ebb and flow of money has helped me tremendously. The more I learn to trust the ebb and flow of money, the freer I am to stay on my path and experience financial success.

Do you trust the ebb and flow of money? For example, do you feel just as comfortable paying bills as you do receiving income?

_____

_____

_____

Do you give money power over you? For example, do you scare yourself by thinking you might run out of money? Or not have enough money to live?

_____

_____

_____

_____

_____

How can you learn to trust the ebb and flow of money? For example, can you make the decision to trust that money will flow to and from you naturally? Do you need to spend less or save more in order to get the flow of money into balance?

_____

_____

_____

_____

> **_I trust the ebb and flow of money._**

Practice Patience

It is so hard for me to be patient! I hate it sometimes. I want to know now that this business will succeed. It's moments like these that I am reminded that I need to practice patience.

Patience is important to launch and grow a business. Patience helps us learn to go with the flow and let the process of entrepreneurship unfold. Sometimes things will happen right when we want them to happen and other times we will need to be patient. Patience helps us trust the process.

There are many opportunities to practice patience. The most effective time to practice patience is when we least feel like it. This experience helps us strengthen our ability to be patient. I practice patience when I am in a traffic jam and when I am standing in line at a grocery store. In these two scenarios, impatience is a natural response for me. In order to practice patience, I make a conscious effort to remain calm and talk calmly to myself saying things such as, "I am patient. This is a good opportunity for me to practice my skills at being patient." If I am in the car, I find a song I like on the radio. My main goal in practicing patience is to stay calm. Remarkably, it works. Wait until you try it!

Look for situations when are you least patient. What situations in your life provide you with the opportunity to practice patience? Are you impatient while waiting in line for a teller at a bank? Waiting in a traffic jam? Describe situations when you are least patient.

1. _____

2. _____

3. _____

4. _____

5. _____

Select one of the areas you've written above to practice patience and describe below how you will consciously practice patience when you are in this situation. Make a conscious effort to practice patience the next time you feel impatient. You may choose to make this a new habit and to practice patience in all of the areas that you are normally impatient. Remember, we can learn to become patient. How will you practice patience?

_____

_____

_____

I practice patience and thus I am patient.

Experience Humility

Tears are flowing through me as I surrender to this process of trust. I've tried to do it my way for so long when all I had to do was trust and believe that I was going to be OK. I finally believe and trust.

Humility is the ultimate surrender to the time before the money flows. It is when we get to this point in our journey that we know we are almost through this time. We usually don't experience humility until we have truly given up every conceivable way to try to do things our way. When we experience humility we are anchored in trust and belief in our path and journey.

I like to use an analogy of the ocean to relate the experience of humility that we encounter along our entrepreneurial journey. When we first start out on our entrepreneurial journey, it is as if we are trying to go out to sea but do not know how to swim. So we learn to swim – but we never swam in the ocean before. We don't know what to expect or what it will be like, so we rely on our swimming skills that we learned. We go to the shore and we begin to swim. Often, the waves will be difficult to swim over and we will be brought back to shore. We make another attempt and another to swim out to sea. Each time we head out to sea, we learn new ways to deal with the waves. Over time, we learn which waves we need to swim under and which waves we need to swim over until we can finally swim out to sea and reach the natural current in the ocean. Once we reach this natural current, we discover something new – that we don't need to swim anymore. We need to learn a new skill now – we need to float. We need to let the current take us where we need to go. It is when we finally reach the current and give up the skill we learned, swimming, and simply float, that we experience humility.

As with the analogy above, we can't force humility nor can we just go there. We need to experience it in our own way and in our own time. Often, the experience of humility is a form of acceptance and may be felt with tears or some other emotion. When we experience humility we can be assured that we are on the right path.

You will experience humility when you trust that you are where you are meant to be. This is when we are best able to trust that we are on the right path. During this time, we are most open and most receptive to any areas of our lives that need to be enhanced or accepted. Just like the swimmer needed to learn how to find the current by swimming and then learn how to float when he/she got there, we need to experience humility to continue on our journey.

This experience, as with many of the experiences we will have in entrepreneurship, is about "oneness" with ourselves and relationships with others. It is about totally surrendering to the process – totally trusting the process.

When we journey into entrepreneurship, we give up something to receive something. Just like the swimmer thought he needed to swim to stay in the sea and discovered that swimming was only important in the beginning of his journey, we need to discover what it is we need to experience in order to stay on our journey. There is humility in consciously knowing what we are giving up in order to become an entrepreneur without knowing what it is we will receive.

I have worked with many clients who have come to experience humility. Often humility comes into our lives when we give up our will and our way of thinking things need to be done. We surrender to the process and begin to trust. Humility is often felt through tears or a sense of giving up on our will – the way we thought or expected things to happen. Humility helps us stay in the "current" of our lives, gets us into the flow, gets us on track.

What does humility feel like to you? Look for areas in your life that you have totally surrendered to. For example, I have tried to build my business as a consultant to major companies in every conceivable way. While I had a few consulting jobs, my business grew in business counseling – helping small business owners in their entrepreneurial journey. When I surrendered to my entrepreneurial journey, I discovered that not only was I a business counselor but an author. Describe the experience of humility in your life.

_____

_____

_____

_____

_____

_____

I welcome the experience of humility.

Develop Your "Rhythm"

I realize that I now beat to the rhythm of my own drum. It took me a while to find my "beat" but for the most part, I find it by listening to myself. If I'm too tired, I rest. I only work when I want to and feel like it – and I am most productive that way.

One of the beautiful aspects of working on our own is that we have the opportunity to develop our own rhythm – to work at a pace and create a schedule that works for us. Developing our rhythm helps us trust that we are on the right path.

We may be used to a rhythm that was set for us – be at the office by 8 a.m., take a lunch break at noon, work until 6 p.m., etc. We have the flexibility now to develop a schedule that works for us. Allow your rhythm to develop. The old work schedule may not be effective in your new work environment. Plus, you have the opportunity to create a schedule that works for you. How fortunate!

Developing your rhythm includes every aspect of your personal and professional life, not just when you work. You may enjoy exercising at 7 a.m. several days a week and start working at 10 a.m. on those days. You may choose to spend one day off in the middle of the week and work on Saturday instead.

Be aware that you may create the same schedule that you had as an employee, including creating all the stress that you felt as an employee. We will recreate the similar circumstances if we are not aware and take the opportunity to learn a new way.

Describe your rhythm. When do you like to work? How often do you need a break? When are you most productive? For example, I am most productive in the mornings and save the less mind-intensive work for late afternoons or evenings. I like to take short breaks throughout the day.

_____

_____

_____

What influences your rhythm? What helps you feel creative and productive when you need to be? For example, I like to write at my kitchen table or out on the porch that looks out over the lake.

_____

_____

_____

I am developing a rhythm that is uniquely mine.

Creating Your Success Path

I realized tonight that I need to change my definition of success. My idea of success has been to run a large profitable company with a lot of employees. The problem is that I do not desire to run this kind of firm – so I don't feel like a success. One of my goals is to create my own definition of success.

Once we understand what is important for our success, we are on the way to creating a success path. A success path is a path that has markers – indicators – that let you know where the path is and whether you are on it. If you have ever traveled in winter when it is snowing, you see markers on the side of the road that let you know you are on the road even though the road is covered with snow. A success path with markers is similar – we may not be able to see the path but we know we are on it.

Our markers help us stay on our success path by reminding us what is important. They represent our definition of success. Think of them as signs as you drive down a road. They can be questions that you ask yourself daily to insure you are on track, they can be affirmations that you are working to believe or they can be a combination of things that help you know you are going in the right direction. Just like you wouldn't get on the highway when you see a "Wrong Way" sign, you can learn to respect your success markers and trust that they are taking you in the right direction. Regardless of what kind of marker you use, if they reflect your definition of success, they will help you stay on the path and gently guide you back onto the path if you get off.

The challenging aspect of using markers initially may be learning to trust them and take appropriate action when necessary. We need to accept that we may initially want to forget about creating a success path and do whatever it was we always did. It is during this time that we need to remember that if we do the same thing, whatever that is, we will get the same results. Remember, just like we trust that the markers on the snow-covered road show where the road is, we can trust that our markers will help guide us on our success path.

We must be willing to identify whatever it is about ourselves that takes us off the path. For example, worry takes me off my success path. One of my success markers is freedom from worry. If I am free from worry or am worried less than I was the day or week before, then I am on my success path. If I get lost in worry, then I immediately know that I have gotten off the path – even temporarily. Our goal is to spend as much time on our success paths as possible so we can experience greater levels of success.

Create questions that you can ask yourself daily to use as your success markers. Use these markers to help you determine if you are on your success path. For example, some of my markers are: Am I feeling good about myself? Did I take action that helped me feel confident? Do I trust myself? Did I remain free from fear and worry? Did I treat myself well? Did I trust and follow my intuition? Did I spend time nurturing my spiritual well being? Did I exercise? Did I trust the process of letting my business unfold today? What coincidences showed up today that helped me know that I am on the right path? Once you create your success markers, use them daily to help you stay on your success path.

1. _____

2. _____

3. _____

4. _____

5. _____

6. _____

Look back over the success markers you created and make sure that you addressed mental, emotional, spiritual and physical aspects. Society typically measures success from a physical standpoint – a big house, a nice car, financial gains. This is not a balanced view of success. Mental success, for example, is acknowledging yourself for all the work you have done to get to this point. Emotional success is recognizing all the progress you made – such as dealing with uncertainty. Spiritual success is continually strengthening your relationship with your higher self.

I learned from this exercise that I did not have success markers that were balanced. I had a limited view of success. I only thought of success in the physical sense. Until I expanded my understanding and view of success, I had a difficult time feeling successful – especially before the money flowed.

Use the space below to add additional success markers to create a balanced success path.

1. _____

2. _____

3. _____

4. _____

5. _____

6. _____

I am creating my success path.

Experience Success Daily

*I am experiencing success daily. I feel good most of the time.
And to think that for years I was looking outside myself for that
feeling when I had the opportunity to experience it the entire
time.*

To experience success daily, we must become unconditionally successful. We do this by deciding what is important to us and then taking appropriate action. We define success internally, not externally. When we feel successful within ourselves, we can trust that money will flow to us. Instead of correlating success to money or to a house, car, job or anything outside ourselves, we need to correlate success to experiencing the fullness of our lives. If we feel good, we feel successful and thus experience success. This concept has worked wonders for me and has been a driving force in helping me take responsibility for my actions, my life and myself. Feeling successful is actually in our control when we take on the new responsibility of doing things or thinking thoughts that make us feel good.

Sometimes we want to look outside ourselves to experience success. We want to see the money come in or the customers come in and that is not happening yet. Especially before the money flows, it is important to look for success in our lives every day. Success is experienced in many ways – when we break through an old pattern of behavior, make a change for the better, feel energy and excitement, or let go of fear and worry. We can experience success throughout our day, not just when we make a big sale or get a new customer. We learn many lessons before the money flows and one of them is to experience success in all we do. Success is to be experienced within ourselves first, and then it will materialize in our physical world.

For example, for years while I was busy trying to feel successful by making more money, I had the desire to spend more time with my father but didn't. I always felt bad about not spending time with him. Once I acknowledged that spending time with my father was important for me to feel good about myself, I started taking actions that were consistent with that desire – spending time with him, feeling good and feeling successful in doing what was important to me.

When we expand our definition of success to define what is important to us and combine that with action, we will experience unconditional success. We will no longer need to seek or gain approval outside of us to feel successful. It is this process of expanding our understanding of success that we expand our knowledge of ourselves. As we continue to grow and trust, our understanding of success will continue to change and become clearer and even more defined.

What makes you feel good? What is really important to you? Spending time with family? Helping others through your work? Creating your work? Living where you want to live? Living the way you want to live? Take your time answering these questions and use your journal if you need to. It is in answering these questions that we define success. Answer these questions over time. Let your definition of success unfold. Trust the process. The answers help us gain greater insight into unconditional success.

_____

_____

_____

_____

_____

_____

What does unconditional success mean to you? For example, I am unconditionally successful in living my life according to my values.

_____

_____

_____

_____

When we recognize success daily, we begin to trust our progress and see our growth. We become acutely aware of just how far we have traveled on this journey. Our daily successes help us trust that we are on course, on our success path. Each success that we recognize and acknowledge moves us farther along our journey, just like a kayaker moves farther along his journey with each stroke.

We can acknowledge our successes by taking time to reflect on our progress. We may take this time when we meditate, write in our journal or talk with supportive friends. What many of us come to discover is that we are the success we've been looking for. The success was within ourselves all along and perhaps we didn't recognize it. We come to learn that no matter what happens on our entrepreneurial journey, we will experience success. We have experienced and trusted the process and we have grown. Our daily successes are like the lights on our path. Each success shines upon us so we can see our next step.

Share your daily successes for the next week. Write at least three successes per day. Get used to looking for daily successes and feeling fulfilled from having experienced each success. Look for situations in your life where you can see progress in terms of your energy, excitement and focus. If you have made progress in any way by being brave, listening to yourself, changing your behaviors, overcoming an obstacle, breaking through a fear, feeling uncomfortable feelings, trusting the progress, this is success! Consider the following questions: What did you do that you felt good about? What did you enjoy? What did you do that scared you? What did you do differently today?

Day 1: _____

_____

_____

_____

_____

Day 2: _____

_____

_____

_____

_____

Day 3: _____

_____

_____

_____

Day 4: _____

_____

_____

_____

Day 5: _____

_____

_____

_____

Day 6: _____

_____

_____

_____

Day 7: _____

_____

_____

_____

I experience success daily.

BEFORE THE MONEY FLOWS
CHALLENGE REVIEW

This challenge provides opportunities to trust the process and experience success in all that you do and in all that you are. The main goal of this challenge is to broaden your perspective of success and trust that the true measures of success are within you.

What did you learn about success by working through this challenge? For example, in writing this chapter, I learned more about trusting the process and letting my life and success path develop instead of trying to make everything happen through my own will.

_____

_____

_____

_____

Is there anything new that was revealed to you as a result of working through this challenge? For example, I realized how grateful I am for having come this far on my journey. I trust that I am where I am meant to be and that I am successful simply by being me and experiencing the fullness of my life.

_____

_____

_____

How do you feel having worked through this challenge? Do you feel you are on your success path, or that you need to make changes or adjust your thinking about success? For example, I feel grounded having worked through this challenge. I feel like I have a greater trust in myself and in the process. I am aware now of how I previously had a limited view and understanding of success.

Have you had any new experiences where you recognized that you handled money situations differently or your understanding of success was expanded? For example, when I paid bills after doing this challenge, I didn't feel the usual pit in my stomach. I decided to trust the flow of money to me and from me. This was a new experience for me.

> **That man (woman) is a success
> who has lived well, laughed often, loved much
> and gave the best he (she) had.**
>
> **Robert Louis Stevenson**

Epilogue

I feel honored to have shared these challenges, opportunities, exercises and experiences with you. Take what you've learned and incorporate it into your lifelong journey. You have come a long way.

The lessons you learned ran deep. Each challenge strengthened core components of entrepreneurship – you learned many lessons that will help you on your journey.

My challenge as well as yours is to maintain the progress we've made and to continually expand ourselves on our entrepreneurial journeys. We know now that we can change and continually improve our lives.

One of the greatest realizations I had in writing this book is that successful entrepreneurship is synonymous with successful living. The more fulfilled we are in our lives, the more success we experience in our entrepreneurial journey.

To learn more about many of the entrepreneurs featured in this book, visit my Web site, www.profit-strategies.com.

Sincerely,

Suzanne

My next book will be a daily affirmation book for entrepreneurs. Watch for it!

Suzanne provides workshops and retreats for entrepreneurs. If you are interested in attending a retreat or workshop or booking one for your organization, contact her. She would also love to hear about your experience with entrepreneurship.
Suzanne@profit-strategies.com.

INDEX

About the Author

Suzanne Mulvehill, MBA is a professional speaker, writer and consultant. As president of Profit Strategies, a company inspiring marketing and development excellence, Suzanne helps entrepreneurs achieve greater levels of personal and professional success. Suzanne is the mother of two, and lives in Delray Beach, Florida, with her daughter, Melissa.